NEWCASTLE/BLOODAXE POETRY SERIES: 6

DESMOND GRAHAM:
MAKING POEMS AND THEIR MEANINGS

NEWCASTLE/BLOODAXE POETRY SERIES

NEWCASTLE/BLOODAXE POETRY LECTURES

In this innovative series of public lectures at the University of Newcastle upon Tyne, leading contemporary poets speak about the craft and practice of poetry to audiences drawn from both the city and the university. The lectures are then published in book form by Bloodaxe, giving readers everywhere the opportunity to learn what the poets themselves think about their own subject.

NEWCASTLE/BLOODAXE POETRY SERIES: 6

DESMOND GRAHAM

Making Poems and Their Meanings

NEWCASTLE / BLOODAXE POETRY LECTURES

BLOODAXE BOOKS

Copyright © Desmond Graham 2006, 2007

ISBN: 978 1 85224 761 4

First published 2007 by
Department of English Literary & Linguistic Studies,
University of Newcastle,
Newcastle upon Tyne NE1 7RU,
in association with
Bloodaxe Books Ltd,
Highgreen,
Tarset,
Northumberland NE48 1RP.

www.bloodaxebooks.com
For further information about Bloodaxe titles
please visit our website or write to
the above address for a catalogue.

Bloodaxe Books Ltd acknowledges
the financial assistance of
Arts Council England, North East.

LEGAL NOTICE
All rights reserved. No part of this book may be
reproduced, stored in a retrieval system, or
transmitted in any form, or by any means, electronic,
mechanical, photocopying, recording or otherwise,
without prior written permission from Bloodaxe Books Ltd.

Requests to publish work from this book
must be sent to Bloodaxe Books Ltd.

Desmond Graham has asserted his right under
Section 77 of the Copyright, Designs and Patents Act 1988
to be identified as the author of this work.

Cover design: Neil Astley & Pamela Robertson-Pearce.

Cover printing: J. Thomson Colour Printers Ltd, Glasgow.

Printed in Great Britain by
Bell & Bain Limited, Glasgow, Scotland.

Contents

I *Opening the Door*

'I like to think of myself as a poet'
(Isaac Rosenberg)

1

My title for this lecture is from one of the many epigraphs prefacing David Jones' Great War narrative poem *In Parenthesis*. For my prologue to this series of three lectures, I will start with his ending, the uncompromising final words of his poem: 'The geste says this and the man who was on the field...and the man who wrote the book...the man who does not know this has not understood anything.' We are left in no doubt of the writer's authority (I quote the words in full, the gaps indicated by the three dots are his own): the man who wrote the book says 'this', as does the man who was there, 'on the field', and the book itself, the 'geste' or poetic history. No room is left for negotiation. Few stronger assertions of poetic authority can ever have been made at the end of a work. To what does 'this' refer, however; what is it that the 'geste' says and we need to know in order to understand anything? The immediately preceding context in Jones' narrative does not really help: there he has just told of new recruits, younger men, coming in the night to replace those dead on the battlefield. These lines make far too general a claim to refer simply to that event. Having been warned that we, as readers, will otherwise know nothing, we ponder, shaken perhaps by the scale of his claim and by his placing us so thoroughly as ignorant outsiders unless we listen.

Such is the way with all poems and our reading of them. We are told something of the utmost importance yet it has none of the firmness or security we would normally expect from a statement outside a poem: simultaneously, in a poem we hear the most demanding claim for public attention (listen – this is true) and a denial of conclusion, as if all the words within the

7

poem surround themselves in invisible quotation marks. The non-linear temporal process which makes up our reading of a poem – going back to the poem, recalling it, discussing it, re-shaping it in our minds, misremembering it, appropriating it – is similar to the non-linear temporal process in which, literally, most poems are written. Notes or jottings or bits and pieces of memory or thought, perhaps carried around for years, lead the poet to a first draft which may have all the material of the future poem or little of it. Other drafts may follow, working on revisions of word and phrase, on metre, if that is present, on rhythm and sound-values and layout, title and visual presentation. After all this there will probably be differing versions of the whole over a further period of time. Modern editors are dubious about the term "definitive" edition: so many poems exist in differing, seemingly complete and seemingly authoritative, versions. In the case of posthumously published work, the presentation of numerous versions has become a common editorial practice.

The process of writing runs across complex and, in the end, unrecoverable time scales in other, non literal senses; unrecoverable at least, until the neurological study of the brain has greatly developed. Words slip and slide and change once they enter a poetic text. We can see clearly in this extreme example, the sorts of thing which can happen. Jones chooses not to deploy quotation marks, but the archaic 'geste' and the rows of dots suggest that the words of his text are an abbreviated quotation. In fact, his published text follows them with a number in super-script, '48', (the real final word of his main text), which directs us to an endnote. In a literal sense then, in this case the last words do not actually finish his book but send us beyond it, to a source, another text, an origin, which will bring its own extending tracks. Some of these tracks we will follow later to see how far we can go to discover what that 'this' may mean. For the present, however, we can observe that the endnote gives evidence of extensive tampering with any notionally "original" source: the lines, in origin, were French, in Ronsard's *Chanson de Roland*; the actual words used here are René Hague's, from his translation of Ronsard into English (a translation which, on inspection, proves to be pretty free). Then in selecting from them and leaving out some of the words, Jones has ensured that they are not really Hague's at all, but something he has made from them. The words Jones has printed in his text are his, but they are derived from a composite effort, selected by him, referring back to their uses elsewhere and their existence across linguistic, cultural and historical time. What Jones is doing is an extension of the kinds of transformations which will take place whenever words are brought into poems. With them they will bring half echoes of previous contexts, other things we have heard or read or can look up; associations and memories of other usages which may, of course, be quite different in the mind of the poet and the mind of the reader and, in turn, differ greatly from reader to reader. The extent to which the poet exerts control over these differences, attempting to direct the reader to specific lines of thought or memory, or attempting to leave as many of these lines as open as he can, will be at the centre of the poet's art, whether consciously or not. The 'Unheard Prompter' of my second lecture will guide him – the patterns and silent punctuation of aural rhythms, metre and other aural effects – as well as choice of word and phrase and structure. The politics of the poet's control over meaning will be the subject of my final lecture. For now, I will move back to simpler though often overlooked things: where do poems come from and how is their making nourished?

2

North Africa, 1943: a young officer, recently rather excited by his experiences in a tank regiment during the desert campaign, more interested in girls and adventure than in literary scenes, receives his post. He replies: 'Dear Tambimuttu – I have just received a letter from a secretary of yours whose name is illegible …and a request for poems. I am sending you some. There are more, if I hear that you have received these and want more' [*Letters*, p. 281].

Tambi, the important, chaotic and charming editor from London's Fitzrovia in wartime had come across two poems published by Keith Douglas in a university magazine of May 1939, *Fords and Bridges*. Tambi had been so impressed by them, he had sought out the author, finally managing to reach the poet's mother in July 1942. He gained her permission to publish poems by Douglas in the magazine he edited, *Poetry (London)*, and in the anthologies he was editing for a series from Faber and Faber, and asked her to send him any future poems she received from her son. True to his word, Tambi published work by Douglas for the third time in the January 1943 issue of *Poetry (London)*.

Now, on 1 June, the same day as he replied to that letter from Tambi's secretary, Douglas sent airgraphs of six poems to *Poetry (London)*. Most had been written in February during his recovery and convalescence from a wound received in the desert fighting. Tambi responded to them on 28 June, asked him for more poems and added: '*Also* would you care to make a selection of your poems for possible publication by PL (Nicholson and Watson) in book form? I think a book by you would be interesting. I hope you will include as many ME poems as possible.' [*Miscellany*, pp.124-25] Douglas accepted, and with his acceptance of 11 July he sent back a new poem 'Aristocrats'. In the next four months before he sailed for England he sent back 'How to Kill', 'Enfidaville', 'Behaviour of Fish in an Egyptian Tea Garden', and had a draft of a new poem called 'A Dead Gunner' which was to become '*Vergissmeinnicht*'.

Tambimuttu's direct encouragement and active help after reading two poems in a university publication was a part, possibly a crucial part, of the creative sources for these poems. He played this part despite the malicious gossip and fictions that can beset the reputations of editors – before hearing directly from Tambi, Douglas had written of an acquaintance '[he] writes for Tambimuttu – who, it appears is Senegalese and a complete shit' (Tambi was from Ceylon not Senegal, and therefore 'Sinhalese'). He had for some time known from his mother that Tambi was publishing his work in the magazine. A second letter he wrote on 11 July gives his own view of the matter: 'Dear Tambimuttu – Thank you for your letter and for publishing my poems – I had given up all idea of writing in the Army until your efforts and John Hall's nerved me to try again.' [11 July 1943, *Letters*, p. 291] Now Douglas writes with confidence of work to be made: 'I'll go on sending you poems as they come – I send you one, "Aristocrats", with this.' Just two weeks before he had written differently, sending poems to John Hall: 'Dear John – ...Did you ever receive the poems I wrote in hospital? I am not likely to produce anything but virtual repetitions of these, until the war is cleared up now, because I doubt if I shall be confronted with any new horrors or worse pain, short of being burnt up, which I am not likely to survive.' [26 June 1943, *Letters*, p. 289]   Spurred by the publisher's enthusiasm and offer to publish a collection, Douglas completed poems he had left in draft and wrote new work which was far from being repetitive of his first batch of war poems. His preoccupation had been with the battlefield's dead: now, it was the morality of the killing and the duality of the soldier's place as both the one who kills and the one who is killed.

Encouragement, attention, publication, a public place for display are the living element of the writer. How else can we allow our work to appear in magazines where we read with a shudder the poems accompanying our own? (Douglas himself, left no record of praise for the contents of *Poetry (London)*). Why otherwise do we find in retrospect that acceptance slips or commissions from an editor whose judgements we do not generally value, actually led to a more productive period of writing than had come from the measured praise and apology for inaction from someone whose judgement we value highly? This may not often affect what the poet specifically writes; it does often greatly affect whether the poet keeps on with writing. This is the outer world of poetry. Some poets need it more than others; some thrive more on adversity, enjoying, like poor footballers, the creative thrust of a managerial boot or tea cup flung across the room; some thrive on distraction and activity; some on seclusion. All are greatly assisted by, even dependent upon, recognition; preferably from someone who can get things done. This dependence, in terms of the survival and recovery of their work, will remain as true after the writer's death, when the scholar and scholarly editor will join with the poets of subsequent generations, literary journalist and publishers, to bring the work to life.

3

The story of Craiglockhart is better known than understood: Sassoon and Rivers, Sassoon and Owen, Owen and Sassoon. It is a story made from memoirs, re-presented in Letters, these letters published posthumously; made from published Diaries (from one side) and biographies (various); add in novels, plays, television drama documentaries and then film and you will know the picture. Behind all this, there is the background story of both men being seen against an already established national myth-like figure and his work, Rupert Brooke. In turn, the story of Owen and Sassoon takes over and adapts this myth of the war poet, just as during the Second World War Owen's own anti-war poetry was absorbed and transformed by the war effort, being presented as evidence not of the horrors of war but of the height of courage found by the soldier to survive in such a world.

What takes us to Craiglockhart here, however, is a different matter: the fact that Owen could not write war poetry until he had read Sassoon. He could certainly write "war prose":

My dug-out held 25 men tight packed. Water filled it to a depth of 1 or 2 feet, leaving say 4 feet of air.
One entrance had been blown in and blocked.
So far, the other remained.
The Germans knew we were staying there and decided we shouldn't.
Those fifty hours were the agony of my happy life.
Every ten minutes on Sunday afternoon seemed an hour.
I nearly broke down and let myself drown in the water that was now slowly rising over my knees.
Towards 6 o'clock, when, I suppose, you would be going to church, the shelling grew less intense and less accurate: so that I was mercifully helped to do my duty and crawl, wade, climb and flounder over No Man's Land to visit my other post. It took me half and hour to move about 150 yards. [...]
In the Platoon on my left the sentries over the dug-out were blown to nothing. One of these poor fellows was my first servant whom I rejected. If I had kept him he would have lived, for servants don't do Sentry Duty. I kept my own sentries halfway down the stairs during the more terrific bombardment. In spite of this one lad was blown down and, I am afraid, blinded.
This was my only casualty. [16 January 1917, *Letters*, pp. 427-28]

This letter was written within days of his first experience of trench fighting and barely two weeks after his arrival in France. His poems trailed far behind. In April, three months after this letter, the promising idea of making a poem about using the gift of an identity disc to commemorate love, leads Owen to write a travesty of a Keatsian sonnet. From the Casualty Clearing Station in May ('*Some* of us have been sent down here as a little

12

mad. Possibly I am among them' [p. 454]) Owen sent his mother the poem 'Sunrise'. It opens: 'Loomed a pale Pearl more marvellous than the Moon's, / Who thereby waned yet wanner than she was...' [p. 456]. In July, arrived in Craiglockhart, he writes to his poet friend Leslie Gunston of working on 'The Ballad of Lady Yolande' – and includes a poem, 'The Fates': 'Those constables called Fortune, Chance and Death; / Time in disguise as one who serves and waits, / ...Escape? There is one unwatched way: your eyes, / O Beauty! Keep me good that secret gate.' A fortnight later, lines Owen quotes from his 'Antaeus' offer blank verse in the manner of Keats's *Hyperion*, which Owen signs, not inappropriately 'Wilpher d'Oen' [p. 477]. What he calls 'the best lines, methinks' from that poem in progress, writing again to Gunston, tell how 'the blood of June glutted his heart. / And all the glow of huge autumnal storms / Stirred on his face' [p. 478]. Certainly Owen is here developing the elegiac mode he greatly valued and never left; and, just as certainly, these poems and most obviously 'Antaeus', with its depiction of male bodies wrestling, reveal a great deal about Owen and where he was as a person. The poems use words, however, in a way which leaves behind their physical, material denotative values even when employed on visual depiction.

In 'Antaeus' the 'blood' of June has no more to do with the blood he saw in France that January than the 'Fatal ordnance' of his poem 'The Fates' had to do with the fatal ordinance which almost drove him to suicide in the dug-out the previous January. In prose, he has no such problem with the shape-shifting, anarchic potential within words: 'Three quarters dead, I mean each of us three quarters dead, we reached the dug-out'; 'I was chiefly annoyed by our own machine guns from behind. The seeng-seeng-seeng of the bullets reminded me of Mary's canary'; 'To call it [No Man's Land] "England". I would as soon call my House (!) Krupp Villa, or my child Chlorina-Phosgena' [p. 429]. Experience of the trenches darkened, deepened and transformed his awareness of language but not in his poems. That is, until he had read Sassoon.

'I have just been reading Siegfried Sassoon, and am feeling at a very high pitch of emotion. Nothing like his trench life sketches has ever been written or ever will be written. Shakespere reads vapid after these. Not of course because Sassoon is a greater artist, but because of the subjects, I mean.' [15 August 1917, pp. 484-85] A week later: 'I have beknown myself to Siegfried Sassoon. Went in to him last night (my second call) ...After leaving him I wrote something in Sassoon's style...' [22 August 1917, p. 485]. The poem, 'The Dead Beat', follows: 'He dropped, more sullenly, than wearily, / Became a lump of stench, a clot of meat, / And none of us could kick him to his feet. / He blinked at my revolver, blearily.' Crude this may be, over-calculated and roughly made; in the succeeding stanzas it was to get worse, as Sassoon observed when he read the draft next day: Owen reports – 'He was struck with the 'Dead Beat', but pointed out that the facetious bit was out of keeping with the first and last stanzas. Some of my old Sonnets didn't please him at all...' [p. 486]. The poem was barely a night's work and already it was Sassoon's critical contribution which was to be crucial; and it was, after all, another example of Owen's attraction to pastiche. What an effect, though, the new model has already had.

With the trench scene for subject, Owen's language within a poem finds immediately what we are persuaded to take as direct observation, 'more sullenly, than wearily'. The first of the epithets 'sullenly' establishes the view of an onlooker, someone narrating the story. Having found in Sassoon's writing a subject – the trench scene – Owen has also found that the mood and charac-ter of the narrator can be as much the matter of a poem as the scene it shows. Shocking the reader with ugliness and insensi-tivity may be the effect he desires, but the most discomforting thing for the reader is the fact that poet fully implicates him-self in the narrator's callousness: none of 'us' (not 'them') could 'kick him to his feet'; it is 'my revolver' which the man blinks at, blearily. The word 'blearily', occasioned by Owen's desire for a full rhyme, sounds a little contrived; yet he has found a word which sustains our awareness of the chilly gaze of this officer's perspective.

Owen would have been able to find such writing in the stories of disdainful British officers trying to bring cringing (or feign-ing) prisoner Albanians, Turks or Germans to pull themselves together in novels by Henty and a dozen others. Through the door Sassoon and his work opened in Owen's poetry, it is made to sound as if it very much comes from Owen's own experience of the trenches. A man dropping, perceived as sullen more than weary; stinking lumps and clots of meat; kicking someone to get them up; the unresponsive and uncomprehending response of blinking eyes and bleary expression – all these Owen would have known. Whether or not he ever aimed his gun at one of his own men, the fact that this weapon is a side arm, designating the narrator as officer threatening one of his own men, would connect with matters of power, responsibility and class which Owen knew too well. As he wrote in that first letter to his mother from the battlefield: a servant he had rejected was killed, the sentry he had posted was blinded, 'This was my only casualty'.

Poem by poem over the next fourteen months, Owen re-wrote Sassoon. Emulation had always been the driving force behind his poetry. He wanted to equal and to be Keats and Milton and Shelley. He wanted to equal and be Sassoon. Now, with Sassoon beside him, making marginal comments, suggesting revisions and titles, rejecting this old work and praising parts of that new piece, he discovered what he could do. At the same time, Sassoon's company gave him the feeling that he had arrived; that his writing had reached past the audience of personal friends and family members only too ready to admire. As a published and established member of a literary world, Sassoon was also able to introduce him and his work to the big outside. Long a poet's poet – a poet communing with dead poets – he had become 'a Georgian'. Emulation, with its shadowy sibling rivalry, led Owen's Sassoon, adoring and grateful as he was, to become greater than the original.

4

Owen's poems were written in Hospital, on Convalescence, on leave or with light duties. The idea of the war poet ducking below the parapet to scribble his great work in indelible pencil is far fetched. As Keith Douglas explained in response to Tambi's request for more new poems:

> I like to write in comfort or not at all and the nearest to comfort available most of the time is not near enough. A few flies are enough to destroy my inspiration, if they keep on the job the way Egyptian, Tripolitanian and Tunisian flies do. What I have written has been

written in hospitals, Con. Depots, Base depots etc – emotion recollected in tranquillity – and as I'm now living in a hole in the sand with a piece of canvas over it, in the inadequate shade of a palm tree, I don't expect to be very creative. I am angling for the job of Brigade Entertainment Officer while we are sitting around, which would enable me to live in a house, with my own room and a vehicle at my disposal. If I get the job I'll send you bags of literature, in all forms and on all subjects. [*Letters*, p. 292]

His confidence is high, he has no lack of recent experience to write about and he has already done work on it, but what he depends on now is good conditions in which to write.

Isaac Rosenberg arrived in France in June 1916. He had printed a couple of pamphlets of his own and was in touch with the poet Laurence Binyon, who was Keeper of Prints and Drawings at the British Museum, Edward Marsh, who was secretary to Winston Churchill and editor of the continuing series of anthologies, *Georgian Poets*, and Gordon Bottomley, whose verse drama Rosenberg greatly admired. With his regiment he moved straight to the Somme trenches and over the next months was in the line or behind it at the '40th Division Salvage Office'. That October he writes to Marsh: 'My dear Marsh: You complain in your letter that there is little to write about; my complaint is rather the other way, I have too much to write about, but for obvious reasons my much must be reduced to less than your little.' [*Works*, p. 248] A little later, perhaps, he writes to Binyon:

It is far, very far to the British Museum from here (situated as I am, Siberia is no further and certainly no colder), but not too far for the tiny mite of myself, my letter, to reach there. Winter has found its way into the trenches at last, but I will assure you, and leave to your imagination, the transport of delight with which we welcomed its coming. Winter is not the least of the horrors of war. I am determined that this war, with all its powers of devastation, shall not master my poeting; that is, if I am lucky enough to come through all right. I will not leave a corner of my consciousness covered up, but saturate myself with the strange and extraordinary new conditions of this life, and it will all refine itself into poetry later on. [p. 248]

Rosenberg had already, in September, sent 'Break of Day in the Trenches' to Harriet Monro who was to publish it that December in *Poetry* (Chicago), along with another army poem of his, 'Marching'. To the heroic resolve of that autumn 1916 letter, he held true, writing poetry whenever he could. After three further months, only sickness relieved him from trench duty; in February 1917 he writes to Bottomley:

> Your letters always give me a strange and large pleasure; and I shall never think I have written poetry in vain, since it has brought your friendliness in my way. Now, feeling as I am, cast away and used up, you don't know what a letter like yours is to me. Ever since November, when we started on our long marches, I have felt weak; but it seems to be some inscrutable mysterious quality of weakness that defies all doctors. [...] I am sending a very slight sketch of a louse-hunt. It may be a bit vague, as I could not work it out here, but if you can keep it till I get back I can work on it then. [pp. 252-53]

The poem is a sketch, though Rosenberg's 'very slight' measures only his ambition and his modesty. 'Louse Hunting' is a wonderful play of disproportionate perspectives – 'See gargantuan hooked fingers / Pluck in supreme flesh / To smutch supreme littleness.' Written presumably at a time of 'some inscrutable mysterious quality of weakness' it carries great energy – 'Nudes – stark and glistening, / Yelling in lurid glee. Grinning faces / And raging limbs / Whirl over the floor one fire' – an energy fuelled by humour and shaped by the visual awareness Rosenberg had developed as a trained, professional painter: 'Soon like a demons' pantomime / The place was raging. / See the silhouettes agape, / See the gibbering shadows / Mixed with the battled arms on the wall.'

By the end of May, Rosenberg was able to send Marsh a draft of his great poem 'Dead Man's Dump'. The conditions under which it was written are not left in doubt by his response to 'criticisms' from Marsh:

> I liked your criticism of 'Dead mans [sic] dump'. Mr Binyon has often sermonised lengthily over my working on two different principles in the same thing and I know how it spoils the unity of a poem. But if I couldn't before, I can now, I am sure, plead the absolute necessity of fixing an idea before it is lost, because of the situation it is conceived in. [...] I have written a much finer poem which I've asked my sister to send you. Don't think from this I've time to write. The last poem is only about 70 lines and I started it about October. It is only when we get a bit of rest and the others might be gambling or squabbling I add a line or two, and continue this way. [27 May 1917, pp. 254-55]

17

The 'much finer poem' he writes of was almost certainly 'Daughters of War'. He was to work on that for the next twelve months. Each opportunity to write, he took; and like Douglas with Tambimuttu and Hall, he was sustained as far as possible by the responses to his work sent by Marsh, Binyon and Bottomley, along with his friend 'Miss Seaton'. For Rosenberg, however, in contrast to Owen, Sassoon and Douglas, a further twelve months of war were not months of recovery, convalescence and time to work on his writing. As a common soldier in a pioneer battalion his life more resembled that of a forced labourer.

> We had a rough time in the trenches with the mud, but now we're out for a bit of a rest, and I will try and write longer letters. You must know by now what a rest behind the lines means. I can call the evenings – that is, from tea till lights out – my own; but there is no chance whatever for seclusion or any hope of writing poetry now. Sometimes I give way and am appalled at the devastation this life seems to have made in my nature. It seems to have blunted me. I seem to be powerless to compel my will in any direction, and all I do is without energy and any interest.
> [To Miss Seaton, 14 February 1918, p. 268]

> I tried to work on your suggestion and divided it ['The Unicorn'] into four acts, but since I left the hospital all the poetry has gone quite out of me. I seem even to forget words, and I believe if I met anybody with ideas I'd be dumb. No drug could be more stupefying than our work (to me anyway), and this goes on like that old torture of water trickling, drop by drop unendingly, on one's helplessness.
> [To Gordon Bottomley, 26 February 1918, p. 268]

> Just now we're out for a rest and I hope the warmer weather sets in when we go up the line again. It is quite impossible to write or think of writing stuff now, so I can only hope for hospital or the end of the war if I want to write.
> [To Rodker, March 1918, p. 269]

Rosenberg had received the latest *Georgian* anthology, with a poem of his in it, along with praise from Bottomley: 'he wrote me there were few pages in the book as beautiful as mine' [p.271]. He hadn't liked much that he read in the book and was now, again, about to move to the front line. He wrote to Bottomley: 'I believe our interlude is nearly over, and we may go up the line any moment now, so I answer your letter straightaway. If only this war were over our eyes would not be on death so much:

it seems to underlie even our underthoughts…I like to think of myself as a poet; so what you say, though I know it to be extravagant, gives me immense pleasure. [7 March 1918, p. 269]

Rosenberg's modest acknowledgement of Bottomley's praise reveals again the importance of such active support to the writer. The scale of the need for confirmation is measured by Rosenberg's unaffected confession, 'I like to think of myself as a poet'. One longs to find humour in these words of his, and puts it there as one reads and re-reads, and then it goes. Yet, on the next day, 8 March, writing to Miss Seaton, Rosenberg moves through a depiction of his difficulties to reiterate his determination:

> I do not feel I have much to say, but you know that unless I write now it will be a long time before you hear from me again, without something exceptional happens. […] Did I send you a little poem, 'The Burning of the Temple'? I thought it was poor, or rather, difficult in expression, but G Bottomley thinks it fine. Was it clear to you? If I am lucky, and come off undamaged, I mean to put all my innermost experiences into the 'Unicorn'. I want it to symbolise the war and all the devastating forces let lose by an ambitious and unscrupulous will.' [pp. 269-70]

Rosenberg's last letter was to Marsh and dated 28 March, it was postmarked 2 April, the day after he was killed. It included, 'just a slight thing': 'Through these Pale Cold Days'; his latest poem.

5

Rosenberg used such time as he had. He did not make it to the time post-war in which he had planned to devote himself fully to writing. Ivor Gurney who did make it by being invalided out, and survived until 1937, beset by increasingly debilitating mental illness, wrote almost all the poems now regarded as his finest work in the mental asylum around 1925-26. This *annus mirabilis* seems to have been brought about by a combination of improved treatment for his illness and the attention of an editor keen to publish his work, J.C. Squire. David Jones only worked on his great poem *In Parenthesis* in the years immediately preceding its publication, 1937. Blunden's finest poems of war were, like Gurney's, mostly written in the early 20s. The importance of time to the making of poems can hardly be overemphasised. It was this emphasis Keith Douglas chose in his last completed poem, sent to his girlfriend at *Poetry (London)* in April 1944, when preparations for the Normandy Landings intensified:

> And all my endeavours are unlucky explorers
> come back, abandoning the expedition;
> the specimens, the lilies of ambition
> still spring in their climate still unpicked:
> but time, time is all I lacked
> to find them, as the great collectors before me.
>
> ('On a Return from Egypt')

Douglas does not leave it there. He closes his poem with a dramatic and characteristic seizing of the initiative with a final stanza which looks to the future. His emphasis upon the need for time, however, is nothing more nor less than the truth. He faces that truth without self pity or false modesty: in comparison with the 'great collectors' before him, time was all he lacked.

Douglas, used the twelve months or so he did have away from the battlefield and without arduous military work to write the poems and prose of war on which his reputation now largely rests. By his return to England in December 1943 he had virtually all his poems of war written and most of his narrative *Alamein to Zem Zem*. What time he had from January to the end of March he spent completing the narrative, making his own illustrations for it, gathering, revising and adding to his poems so as to leave them as a collection, and successfully turning Tambi's promises into contracts to publish. In this, as all who knew him at the time confirm, he was driven by the expectation that he would not survive, and that turn of mind which was damn well going to make sure he made the most of the time he had.

Helped both by the presence of an enthusiastic publisher committed to publishing work, and by his suspicions as to the practical efficiency of that publisher when it came to fulfilling promises, Douglas completed his tasks. He was helped to do so by his unusual lack of interest in literary worlds and the company of writers. He found time, alongside his writing and his military training to fight on mainland Europe, for a last and fulfilling love affair. Whenever he made it to London in early 1944, Tambi's editorial assistant, Betty Jesse, was the target of his attentions. The much written-about bohemian life of Fitzrovia and its pubs which swirled around Tambi had no interest for him.

Douglas was prepared to share the fact of his writing with anyone around him. From the school common room where he told Norman Ilett he had just written a pastiche of Auden which Grigson couldn't resist and would publish in *New Verse* (he was right), through to his giving a fellow patient, John Stubbs, the parody of Rupert Brooke he had just written, while they both recovered from wounds at El Ballah General Hospital, Douglas made no secret of his writing. He sent poems to girl-friends, much as he painted their portraits, if he could, to impress them. With Olga Meiersens, a friend who worked at a Tel Aviv bookshop he talked about his writing and poetry, well into the night. He did not share with anyone the actual process of making his poems: the fellow poet, the friend, critic or lover, or combination of all four, who goes over your drafts with you, who figures so prominently in most poets' lives.

For Owen, Sassoon remained the first three of these (and speculation has not been lacking about how and to what extent and why he not the fourth) and it was to Sassoon that Owen sent 'a few poems to tempt you to a letter', back in France and about to move up to the trenches, late in September 1918 [p.578]. A comment in this letter about remarks he had seen reported in 'the Mail the other day' was to lead to his final poem 'Smile, Smile, Smile'; a wonderfully understated piece, on the soldiers' shared knowledge, which he drafted on the back of a love poem a friend had sent him for comment. In the letter to Sassoon he enclosed a poem he had worked on at Craiglockhart, now called 'The Sentry', which returned to his first experience of the trenches, when the servant he had rejected was killed and he nearly let himself drown. He could well have been prompted to return to that poem by meeting his new acting company sergeant major. The man, as Owen wrote to his mother, 'was a corporal with me in the first dug-out where the Sentry was blinded, you remember. He remembers it...' [p. 584]. His paragraph tails off with these dots.

The speaker of 'The Sentry' is a confident, military man, much as Owen was to depict himself to his mother after the next days of 'sheer' fighting – 'My nerves are in perfect order' [p. 580]; 'I scrambled out myself and felt an exhilaration in baffling the Machine Guns by quick bounds from cover to cover. After the shells we had been through, and the gas, bullets were like the gentle rain from heaven.' [p. 581] Such humour, however, is absent. The narrator of Owen's poem is just a little too obsessive in his detail, too impersonal towards the soldiers under him. The narrator himself is, once more, as much the subject of the poem as the action he describes but the angry exposure of extremity in that first war poem, 'The Dead Beat', is replaced by the portrayal of an officer who is in charge but finds things a bit too much for him. Control is what he aspires to, control of his own story and its confession.

> ...There we herded from the blast
> Of whizz-bangs; but one found our door at last, –
> Buffeting eyes and breath, snuffing the candles,
> And thud! flump! thud! down the steep steps came thumping
> And sploshing in the flood, deluging muck,
> The sentry's body; then his rifle, handles
> Of old Boche bombs, and mud in ruck on ruck.
> We dredged it up, for dead, until he whined,
> 'O sir – my eyes, – I'm blind, – I'm blind, – I'm blind.'
> Coaxing, I held a flame against his lids
> And said if he could see the least blurred light
> He was not blind; in time they'd get all right.
> 'I can't,' he sobbed. Eyeballs, huge-bulged like squids',
> Watch my dreams still, – yet I forgot him there
> In posting Next for duty...

The officer does confess to his haunting, but he wished to assume the manly release of forgetting, so as to find a point of rest: 'Those other wretches, how they bled and spewed, / And one who would have drowned himself for good, – / I try not to remember these things now.' He is impelled to complete his story: 'Let Dread hark back for one word only...' – 'Half-listening to that sentry's moans and jumps, / And the wild chattering of his shivered teeth, / Renewed most horribly whenever crumps / Pummelled the roof and slogged the air beneath, – / Through the dense din, I say, we heard him shout / "I see your lights!" – But ours had long gone out.'

Nothing in the poem qualifies this despair, yet it remains a desperate and unsuccessful attempt by the officer and those he speaks for, to find closure. Behind his impotent and abused authority, we are made to hear questions which won't stop resonating long after his words and the poem are finished.

When Owen first drafted 'The Sentry' he included specific names; 'Another sentry! yours Jacks, up you go' and 'The sentry's body! Jones' [p.372]. Douglas had done the same in the draft of '*Vergissmeinnicht*' he brought with him from North Africa. Comrades killed by anti-tank fire are recalled, 'Bielby', who was killed in April 1943, and 'Evans', killed the previous December. Similarly, the photograph of the girl Steffi, definitely the lover of the dead German gunner in the latest versions, was simply part of the scene in this draft:

> ...(But) they left one,
> they left you, perhaps the boy
> to whom Steffi had written Vergissmeinnicht
> on this photograph in the ditch. Perhaps the hand
> rhat gave Evans and Bielby their last gift
> [*Poems*, pp.xxviii-xxix].

Poems draw directly on experience. Douglas himself advised John Hall as a poet: 'Let your impulses drive you forward; never lose contact with life or you will lose the impulses as well.' [*Poems*, p. 135] But how they draw on experience and which experiences and when, are questions which lead to numerous discoveries but few answers. I will end with three examples from another poet of war, Anna Akhmatova.

As her biographers reveal, more than any other poet perhaps, she wrote her life in her poems and her poems through her life. Each event of her historical times, right through Stalin's terror and the loss of husband and son, is there. Days and nights can be located and placed with accuracy. In her poems, she could write of herself, with justice, as mother Russia, as a statue, a monument, and while doing so, make an art in which we feel that this lover left at this very moment yesterday, this person is one we could meet and ask, this place was just where she was that day. The recent biography by Elaine Feinstein, *Anna of All the Russias*, brings this out persuasively and with great tact. I am indebted to her detail in my examples here.

Akhmatova was from the first surrounded by poets. Her husband, Gumilyov, was a poet. 'The Poets' Guild of Acmeists', which included Osip Mandelstam, gathered at their house. Her first collection was published from Gumilyov's workshop. Gumilyov wrote about the poems, particularly praising the way 'a series of beings, mute until now, had acquired a voice...women in love, cunning and rapturous, at last speak their own genuine and at the same time artistically convincing language'. Akhmatova, Feinstein comments, 'was almost embarrassed by her sudden fame: "I considered it indecent, as if I had left a stocking or a brassière on the table".' The understanding of the implicit sexism in Gumilyov's generous praise is not as important in this case as her awareness that her art has been misunderstood. Feinstein explains: 'She wanted the poems to be read as fictions rather than confessions.' [p. 37] Gumilyov, according to Feinstein, did not make an issue of the confessional tone of her poems whether or not he objected to it: the subject of a poem could be another matter. When she wrote: 'Yesterday my husband beat me / With his woven belt folded double', readers responding to the intimate manner of her work were ready to see this as biographical [p. 39]. Gumilyov, like most poets in my experience (let alone errant husbands) was particularly sensitive to the literal. He did not beat her. The lines offended him.

The very point where to the reader a poem may seem closest to the biography of the poet, may be the point where the poem is furthest from the poet's literal experience. The most telling, and confessional moment, in Wilfred Owen, the one place where he writes directly of killing, is probably the least likely to be drawn from his own direct experience. At the close of 'Strange Meeting', the dead German soldier addresses the poet – 'for so you frowned / Yesterday through me as you jabbed and killed'. This may well come from a nightmare Owen suffered. It may well relate to fears of his and the workings of his imagination during army training. It relates, beyond question, to so much his mind, his memory and his experience of battle carried. As an officer, however, he would have been armed only with a pistol. The likelihood of him having actually bayoneted someone in the trench fighting he had by then experienced is too remote to be worth consideration.

My second example from Feinstein shows the poet herself relating a poem to a specific event. Feinstein writes of how Akhmatova, in exile in Tashkent in 1942, was visited by a Polish soldier and artist, Joseph Czapski, introduced by Alexey Tolstoy.

They spent a miraculous extended evening of talk, during which Czapski translated Polish poems for her, extempore; she read from her own work, including poems about Leningrad which moved him. Seventeen years later, in the cycle of poems 'Tashkent Pages', she recalls the evening:

> We drove one another out of our minds that night.
> The ominous darkness shone as if for us,
> the canals seemed to be murmuring to themselves
> and all the carnations smelled of Asia.
>
> ...
>
> If perhaps you recall this night, in a life
> whose future shape remains hidden from me,
> then simply think these sacred moments once
> returned to a stranger in a dream.

Quoting these two stanzas, Feinstein observes: 'Akhmatova told Chukovskaya that this poem arose after her meeting with Czapski'. I like the wording 'arose after'. It allows this compelling piece from Akmatova as a poet, to remain untouched by Feinstein's next comments: 'In his own memoirs, however, Czapski does not write of walking Akhmatova home, or indeed of spending any time with her alone. His description of Akhmatova as "a rather detached person with whom it was difficult to make contact" hardly suggests intimacy, though he adds, "I should have liked to get to get to know this poet better, see her tête à tête. But I did not dare to pursue the acquaintance".' [p.201] Perhaps Czapski's last words give the game away; whether he is being ungenerous, self-protective, forgetful, brutally or plainly accurate is no matter. The curiosity of such questioning is idle beside the transformation her art performed, the new experience which is made within her poem and given to the reader.

Poems draw on life. How else could the poet write them? But how they draw and what they draw is generally too rich and idiosyncratic, too creatively unreliable to be recoverable. The excitement is how poems twist and lie, how they change and confuse things lived, sometimes literally and, most commonly, beyond the point which even the poets themselves would expect or recognise. The whole creative process is, in the end, only really worth attention to see how unexpected and even bizarre it can be: even to the extent of sometimes being completely literal to the truth.

One of the Leningrad poems Akhmatova might have read to Czapski provides the last of my examples. The poem refers to the siege and heroic resistance, and to the suffering of those she left behind in the city when flown out. It is in two parts, the second an elegy 'In Memory of a Leningrad Boy, my neighbour Valya Smirnov' [*Poems*, p. 151]. Valya Smirnov was Akhmatova's neighbour. He did live in the house next door. One of two little brothers, he did often visit her. She did fly to Tashkent and there she heard the news that his house had been hit during a bombardment and he had been killed.

> Knock with your little fist – I'll open up.
> I always opened my door to you.
> Now I've gone beyond the high mountain,
> the desert, the wind and the blazing heat,
> but I will never give you up...
>
> I did not hear you crying
> or asking for bread
> Bring me a twig from the maple tree,
> or just some blades of green grass
> as you did last spring.
> Bring me in your tiny cupped hands
> some clear, cool water from our Neva,
> and with my own hands I'll wipe clean
> the blood from your little golden head.

II *The Unheard Prompter*

```
x    /   x /  x  /   x   /   x  /
```
'Look **here** / up**on**/ this **pic**/ ture **and** / on this'
(Hamlet)

1

The patterning of sound and emphasis, along with other rhetorical means like repetition, balance and timing has always been used for the listener's pleasure and as a means to persuasion, and not only by poets. Rhetoric and eloquence, historically seen as highly desirable skills and as most suspect means of deceiving have, of course, generally, if not always, been loved by poets. Different fashions will be favoured at different times. The archives of poets' reading styles from Tennyson and Yeats through Eliot and David Jones, on then through Heaney or Harrison to the present, show how poets have wanted their work to be heard in quite different ways at different periods; between, in the broadest scale, the publicly declaimed and the informally spoken. Different writers desire different emphases; even within the writing life of a single writer, the chosen emphases may change. It is not difficult to trace a broad move through Shakespeare's verse, from late/mid sixteenth-century decoration and eloquence to early seventeenth-century expressiveness, or 'roughness' as they might have said; the move from the verse of Marlowe's *Tamburlaine* to that of Donne.

Speaking or singing your own verse you have control through pitch, length and pause – hence the familiar disappointment of wonderful, sung lyrics which look poor and clichéd in print. Writing or publishing verse for others to speak, or for them to read on a printed page, you may well want to develop some system of notation to stop things getting out of hand. In fact, medieval punctuation tried to mark the pauses in delivery rather than the syntactical groupings; it also tried to mark pitch. A text was there to be read out loud so the speaker was given help. Dramatic texts, at least, earlier ones, performed a similar function: printed for the performer of the future or to leave a record of previous performance. Living after St Ambrose's world-changing discovery – silent reading – poets need their written or printed text to indicate as much as possible what the voicing of it would previously have indicated. Today, in composing our poems, some of us mumble to ourselves as we write; some walk around speaking the words; some beat out time on the table: almost all writers at some points in composition say the poem aloud to themselves. For many writers doing this actually generates the poem. It is also a way of checking out meaning and, often in the later stages, checking out the effect of the visual, typographical features – what does that punctuation/lack of punctuation do? What do the line-endings/paragraphing/line-lengths do? In the end, listening to how poems sound, is like the old practice of dropping a coin to hear it ring, listening to find out whether it is fake or sound.

At the one extreme, to hear a poet read his own work can be a revelation, all the queries we had about tone and humour and level of feeling vanish: I remember first hearing Hughes read *Crow*, and the nature of the humour, the ironies, the tone were at once clear. At the other extreme, there is the all too common experience of the poem which the poet, and perhaps their lover, hears as overwhelmingly beautiful while the listener, in love with neither of them, does not: 'I held her hand/and she looked up...' 'Can't you feel this', they ask. 'You must be without feeling not to be moved'. As authors, the poem must sound right to us, but too readily we deceive ourselves by hearing what we want to hear in the poem. The reader can do the same of course, but that matters far less as they are not in charge of revising and shaping the text. For the author then, the second stage is always to try the poem out on others. How does it sound to oneself when we are voicing it to others? How does it sound to them? Even, as is practised in some workshops, how does it sound when they voice it, reading our poem aloud to us? The writer's reaction will depend on how great the disparity they come across; how much they find that reader reliable; and, above all, how much control they actually want over their text.

I am going to look at rhythmical and aural patterns in poems, to show how these can help to compose and potentially control the meaning. Poets often talk in workshops and interviews of wanting 'the poem to be right', 'wanting the poem to sound right', 'wanting to let the poem speak for itself', 'letting the poem find itself'. All such remarks can be seen as vague, evasive, unhelpful. Generally they are, and they can also sound extremely pretentious. With the right tone, however, they are also correct and essential. It is most often at a later stage of composition that poets are consciously concerned with meaning. Of course, they are concerned with meaning each day of their thinking life; they may want to write a poem about this or that; they may have a specific commission; the poem may be part of an extended sequence; they may have strong political views. All such things will underlie the making of the poem. These things may well become part of the conscious shaping as the poet tests out and revises the poem later on. In composing, however, it will be 'getting the poem to sound right' which the poet is likely to follow – 'Why did you change that line?' 'Because it sounded wrong.' 'How did you manage to come up with that phrasing?' 'It seemed right'.

I find such comments far more trustworthy and encouraging from a writer than elaborate explanations, though of course I might disagree with them at each point. Equally, literal questions of meaning often consciously worry a writer far more than elaborate ideas – 'Does a bullfinch move like that?' 'Would you find a dogfish there?' 'If she started from there, how did she get to there?' As far as what is commonly called "meaning" is concerned, most poets I know would share my feeling that I don't want to find, after testing a few readers, that my lines provoke a meaning I don't actually want. At the same time, I would often be hard-pressed to say what was the meaning I did want. The poet can try to cut down what is wrong as far as he is concerned, but it is the poem's job not the poet's, to say whatever is right; whatever that is.

The notion that "sounds" have meaning in themselves, even onomatopoeic sounds, has been discredited for years. That meaning does get attached to sounds within a context is now generally agreed. The well-meaning schoolchild who talks of 'the sound of gunfire in the repeated 'r's of Owen's "rifle's rapid rattle"' is appropriately corrected. The reader who talks of the importance of the sound of the words Owen chooses to describe machine guns beside him, 'The seeng-seeng-seeng of the bullets reminded me of Mary's canary' may well have something interesting to say. Concentration on specific vowels and consonants in Owen's 'Anthem for Doomed Youth', may actually distract from the importance of other patterns, such as the semantic relationship which make up Owen's word-play: 'rattle [to talk on]' 'patter [as in a comedian's]' 'orisons [prayers]', for example: but the poem's elaborate, extensive and detailed play of vowel and consonant sound remains crucial to its own structuring. In such a poem, which simultaneously discredits and re-writes the religious, patriotic, communal song of his title, 'Anthem', the importance of the deployment of sound is hardly surprising.

Physical sounds of words within a printed poetic text are difficult, perhaps impossible to recover or to discuss with much certainty. Each reader and poet will hear a particular variety of the language within their heads, or will voice that variety as they recite or speak the poem – not just English from North America or Ireland or India but an English made from their particular family and cultural background, their education and gender and above all, their historical time. Today we have the useful idea of 'standard English' but not only does the concept vary from place to place, hardly anyone anywhere actually speaks it. In Shakespeare's time there wasn't even the notion of it. There was not even one form aspired to and claimed by a powerful social group. His actors will have spoken their own version of late Elizabethan Geordie or Devonian or Middlesex or Dublin or Dundee English. As he composed his sonnets, was Shakespeare hearing and speaking them in early seventeenth-century Brummagen or Cockney or Hampton Court posh, or some idiosyncratic mix of his own? Fascinating work has been done in trying to reconstruct the versions of English used at his time but of course, London alone, as is the case today, would be full of so many varieties. Shakespeare would have had his own version of whichever variety he was closest to.

All that follows then must be taken with large pinches of salt. My defence is that I am aiming to show that sound can be deployed by the poet not only for pattern but to suggest meaning and guide the reader. My focus will first be on metre and the direction it can give us as to what the poet heard, consciously or not. Attending to metre actually makes the whole task possible. Where rhythm is created by the living sounds of the language as used by poet and reader; where rhythm is an amalgam of numerous overlapping elements – stress and length, pitch and pace, syntax and meaning, lay-out and typography – metre is only notional. It is a notional regular pattern on which the poet can base a poem, and once the pattern is observed, it can be followed or not within the actual rhythms. It is made up of numbers of syllables per line, grouped into units, most commonly of two or three, according to repeated patterns of stressed and unstressed syllables. Metres in poetry in many languages other than English are based on length of syllable, as was much English verse before the seventeenth century. Here I am discussing metrical patterns which are stress based and, specifically, the most common pattern in English, iambic pentameter – ten feet per line, each foot two syllables, the first unstressed, the second stressed.

For the poet, of course, it is the interplay between the metrical pattern which the reader is led to expect, and the actual patterns made by the various components of the rhythm, which proves endless creative excitement. My purpose – to show how the poet can move and shape meanings by listening to this silent pattern and the reader can recover them by attending to it – depends on removing as much contentious and complex material as possible. The metre is not the only element in my examples, not necessarily the most important, but it can lead us to see certain important things which might otherwise remain hidden.

2

Shakespeare's sonnets are a goldmine – and minefield – of word-play: registers, technical language, extended metaphors, puns, jokes and double-entendres are used with endless cunning. Their patterns of sound and syntax are models of great writing; their playing off of metre against rhythm masterly. My first example is simple and, through its simplicity, I hope, keeps at bay unwanted problems. The first four lines of the first of his sonnets are iambic pentameter, five feet to a line, each foot an unstressed syllable followed by a stressed:

From fair/est crea/tures we/ desire/ increase
That there/by beau/ty's rose/ might ne/ver die
But as/ the ri/per should/ by time/ decease
His ten/der heir/ might bear/ his mem/ory

The final foot here, 'ory', indicates how metre is notional; the foot could actually be sounded to rhyme with '**die**', '**mem**/ory', or it could be sounded as just one syllable through an elision, '**mem**/'ry'. Whatever your decision about this individual foot, it will remain part of a poem in iambic pentameter.

Modern readers so often try to come to the metre through what they see as the poem's meaning, locating the words they would choose to emphasise and then marking them as metrically stressed. The opposite is the case. Once established, the metre directs the reader to potential stresses: look for those metrical stresses and you may find where the emphasis lies. In English, as is common in languages, stress on the sounding of a word can give it emphasis, indicating that it has importance and affecting its meaning. Try: 'I came **here**' 'I **came** here' and '**I** came here'. The poet using metre, hearing its patterns as he writes, may well find in it a means of pointing to emphasis, of directing meaning. As the poet writes, the metrical patterns may form an invisible punctuation in his head, may function as intonation does in speech and typeface can do in printing. It will be what the poet hears, making decisions about emphasis which most often will not be conscious but which we register and can retrieve. In the following text I have marked only those places within the regular metre of unstress, stress, which I will discuss: where it is a metrical stress I have used bold type; I have used italic where the syllable is metrically unstressed.

From fairest creatures **we** desire increase
That thereby beauty's rose *might* never die
But as the riper **should** by time decease
His tender heir *might* bear his memory
But **thou**, contracted to *thine* **own** bright eyes...

'**Should**' receives metrical stress in line three: 'But as the riper **should** by time decease'. Thus the assertive aspect of the word is supported, its potential to be tentative underplayed. Through this metrical emphasis the meaning focuses on what ought to be the case, ought to be a matter of course, the normal state of things. In lines two and four the use of 'might' coincides each time with an absence of metrical stress. Thus the potential in 'might' to express reserve or indecision if emphasised (something that could or could not happen) is not introduced. Instead, lacking stress, the word performs a simpler function, meaning 'would never die' or 'would be able to bear his memory'.

Metre is particularly revealing in terms of pronouns. The first 'we' here receives metrical stress. With such emphasis a cluster of meanings can be released: we – as humans, doing what is natural, proper – should desire to procreate. At the same time the emphasis on 'we' releases the word's power to indicate something shared between individuals, between us, we two. Metre is therefore taking part in both the personal, intimate area of the poem's address and the politics of its argument. In contrast, 'his' has no metrical stress in line four, 'His tender heir…': this is not someone in particular, the poet is just giving an instance. Shakespeare then leaves persuasive generalities and turns to direct address, letting the stress fall on the pronoun: 'But thou…'. The tone here may be accusatory, tender, disappointed or in some other mood or combination of moods, but the metre makes clear that it is personal, that it does, brutally or gently, point a finger.

> But thou, contracted to *thine* own bright eyes,
> Feed'st thy light's flame with self-substantial fuel,
> Making a famine where abundance lies,
> *Thy*self *thy* foe, to thy sweet self too cruel.

Stress falls on the pronoun 'thou' but 'thine' is unstressed, metrical stress falling on 'own'. The accusation has been narrowed so as to focus not on the person but the fault, narcissism. From here on, the metrical stresses help to reveal the whole course of the argument, its shifts and emphases. 'Thy' and 'self', are both metrically stressed: they are the terms through which the ensuing debate will take place. In the word-play, repetition, and sound-patterning which carries the last of these lines here – the metre indicates a route through such riddling: 'self' is stressed not 'Thy'; then 'foe' not 'thy': the subject, this insists, is not the person addressed but the issue under debate. Then the emphasis shifts back again with metrical stress, turning personal, 'to thy sweet self': between these stresses the compliment 'sweet' is diminished, half-heard, an attribute of the person addressed but an attribute overwhelmed by that person's fixation on self: 'Thy**self** thy **foe**, to **thy** sweet **self** too **cruel**'. Through the metre's direction, the clever word-play and riddling can impress without distracting from a precise, personally targeted, unmistakeably defined accusation.

The work of metre can be disguised or undone by the efforts of the modern editor, trying to bring the clarity of modern punctuation marks to the earlier text. Reading the opening of the fourth sonnet in Shakespeare's sequence 'Unthrifty loveliness, why dost thou spend / Upon thyself thy beauty's legacy', the insertion of the comma here, before the questioning 'why', may well lead the reader to stress that word '**why** dost thou spend…' where Shakespeare's metre had punctuated for us: 'why **dost** thou **spend** / Upon thyself thy beauty's legacy'. With this metrical stressing of 'dost' and downplaying of 'why' the question asks for an explanation rather than offering a challenge, and the tone of this is likely to sound not so much like dismay as like reasoned enquiry. With this tone, the double-entendre in 'spend upon thyself' at the end of the line, is cunningly covered by an air of reasonableness: surely this isn't suggesting that self-love is akin to masturbation? Modern editors introduce another comma in the next line – 'Nature's bequest gives nothing, but doth lend' – the alteration of emphasis is slight but telling. Metrically there is no pause between 'nothing' and 'but', suggesting, not that nature doesn't give anything but that nature merely lends rather than gives. The last of my examples here is more decisive: a comma is inserted after an initial 'Then' – 'Then, **beaut**eous **nigg**ard…'. Responding to the emphasis the comma suggests, 'Then' sounds over-insistent, pedantic, school-masterly even; without that modern punctuation, punctuating by metre we move swiftly towards the compliment which follows: 'Then beauteous niggard…' – the two epithets carry the same metrical movement from stress to unstress: praise and insult are parallelled, making a praising-insult or insulting praise. The recipient is likely to be left just where the poet wants him, off-balance, unable to be sure whether he is being accused or wooed.

Shakespeare sonnets, of course, are brief scenes of relationship. There is a speaker and an addressee, a wooer and a wooed, lover or friend or both. These opening poems in the sequence set out to persuade: through their skill; through their irresistible mastery of poetic discourse; through their capacity to ask, to complain, to compliment, to woo, to chasten, insult and arouse; and through their ever-shifting balance between impersonal proposition (truth and logic) on the one hand and intimate (emotional, private) knowledge and need on the other. Nuance, delicacy of tone, when to be frank and when veiled, are so important in such an art. Listening to the metre of the sonnets we may hear the voices Shakespeare uses. Ignoring the metre we may depend upon the familiar sounds of our own voice.

In writing for the theatre such metrical direction is more obviously important. Through the metre the poet can direct the actor towards emphasis, mood, tone and implicit punctuation, just as in the sonnets. Through the metre, the listening audience can be directed as to the nature and course of the argument, the movement of the character's speech, and even the stage situation in which it is being spoken. Here is a passage from *Hamlet*. The metre, from the first of its lines, 'Look **here** upon *this* **pic**ture **and** on **this**...', indicates to the audience exactly what Hamlet is pointing out, rather in the manner of some later, plain stage direction – '*He points to the first picture... he takes up a second...*'. Actor and audience are helped to visualise and understand exactly what is being shown on stage. Metrical stress will, as always, point up important words, nouns (like the physical terms in the following speech, '**ear**' and '**eye**' and '**blood**'), and verbs ('**was**' and '**is**'); it is the pronouns again, where stress and lack of stress provide a secret syntax which constructs the mood and direction of Hamlet's address to his mother. (Again I mark the points in the metre to which I am drawing attention with bold type for stresses and italic for un-stresses.):

> Look **here** upon *this* **pic**ture, **and** on **this**...
> *This* **was** *your* **hus**band. **Look** *you* **now** *what* follows.
> *Here* **is** *your* husband, **like** a mildewed **ear**
> Blasting *his* wholesome brother. **Have** *you* **eyes**?
> *You* **can**not **call** it **love**, for **at** *your* **age**
> The heyday in the **blood** is tame, it's humble
> And waits upon the judgement; **and** *what* **judg**ement
> Would step from **this** to **this**? *What* **dev**il was't...
>
> (*Hamlet*, III iv 52*ff*)

The errors Hamlet points out, are not wrong as *her* personal choices, but as actions against what is natural: this was not '**your** husband' but '*your* **hus**band'; he doesn't insist 'have **you** eyes' and 'at **your** age' but '**have** you **eyes**...for **at** your **age**'. The metre underpins the dramatic emphases. It also shows how Hamlet, like the poet of the sonnets, wished to persuade through appeal to general truths and deflect from a response which would see the argument as a matter of personality or occasion.

3

Pronouns could hardly be more important in Wordsworth's *Prelude*. His epic will call as evidence the story of his own experience: that **he** felt or thought or knew something, will prove it to be true. The persuasiveness of this evidence to others will depend upon its appearance of authenticity and accuracy. Where the Shakespeare sonnets I have looked at used the material of personal feeling to add colour, an immediate target and dramatic importance to his arguments, it was the irresistible truth of the arguments themselves which was employed to persuade the hearer and bring home the personal weight of the message. With the opening of the *Prelude*, the method is reversed. The man speaking to men will tell us things about himself which, if we can hear them exactly, will convince of the general truths he wants us to conclude. Nothing in this argument is likely to have more importance than the first person pronoun. Hamlet, soliloquising, can give us a good glimpse of how important that pronoun can sound: 'Yet I...Am I a coward...Swounds I should take it...why what an ass am I...that I the son ...Hum I have heard...'. Each I is re-doubled in strength by being the point of a metrical stress. Hamlet's self here, as the centre of knowledge, manages to strike up the voice of command and, at the same moment, to throw into question the very value of personal, subjective knowledge. Now to Wordsworth: we have to wait until the eighth line of his *Prelude* to reach the first 'I', but in the lines which follow it, none of the subsequent pronouns is backed by stress:

> ...
> Now **I** am **free**, enfranchis'd and at large.
> May **fix** *my* habitation **where** *I* **will**.
> What dwelling **shall** receive *me*? In what Vale
> Shall **be** *my* harbour?

Another metrically stressed 'I' follows, reminding the reader that the choices available to the poet will be subjective, but after that, for six lines the metre offers no supporting stress to any of the nine personal pronouns which follow. The reader may increasingly wish to make the whole thing a story about Wordsworth. The metre insists now, however, that it is what is happening to him that matters, not that it is happening to him rather than someone else:

> ...Underneath what grove
> Shall I take up *my* home, and what sweet stream
> Shall with its murmurs lull *me* to *my* rest?
> The earth is all before *me*: with a heart
> Joyous, nor scar'd at its own liberty
> *I* look about, and should the guide *I* chuse
> Be nothing better than a wandering cloud
> *I* cannot miss *my* way. *I* breathe again;

After that first stressed I, 'Shall **I** take **up** my **home**' the poet has vanished into being the bearer of the story. It is the power of the **stream** to **lull** to **rest**; it is the **earth** which is **all** before him; it is the freedom to **look** about, to **choose** a **guide**, to find the **way**, to **breathe** again, that are important. It will be six more lines before the long sentence started here is completed. At its close, the metrical underplaying of the personal pronouns will be replaced by two stresses, one on '**mine**' and the other on the final word of the lengthy sentence, '**me**':

> Trances of thought and mountings of the mind
> Come fast upon *me*: it is shaken off,
> As by miraculous gift 'tis shaken off,
> That burthen of *my* own unnatural self,
> The heavy weight of many a weary day
> Not **mine**, and such as were not made for **me**.

His case is completed, the evidence has been given and from its argument we can conclude with a powerful awareness of his, subjective identity. The natural world has removed the 'burthen' and 'heavy weight' brought by stultifying surroundings and returned him to his true, natural self.

Brennan O'Donnell, writing with great tact and clarity about Wordsworth's metre, leaves no doubt about how Wordsworth felt on the subject in his chosen title: *The Passion of Metre: A Study of Wordsworth's Metrical Art* (Ohio, 1995). O'Donnell's chapter on the blank verse affirms: 'Wordsworth considered his blank verse a consummate artistic accomplishment. In letters written in his middle and late years, he is quick to admonish correspondents who tend (like many twentieth century commentators) to confound the painstaking fashioning of a powerfully original and various voice in blank verse with artless or 'natural' expression. In a letter of 1831, Wordsworth warns William Rowan Hamilton not to be tempted by the seeming naturalness of blank verse into supposing the effect of effortlessness takes no effort.' [p.179] Naturalness, flexibility and subtle variety are the main elements which O'Donnell shows Wordsworth to have sought consciously in his work on the metrics of his poems. He does not venture into the kinds of local, specific pointing which have been my subject here. My concern has been with how that passion for metre could provide an invisible punctuation, attended to by the poet's ear as he composes and recoverable by the reader in the meanings he makes.

3

Vowel and consonant sound also may contribute to a poem's argument. The numerous forms of echoing and related sounds within a poem, make shapes and patterns which structure it. Again, it is to these the poet will listen as he writes. In the first of the Shakespeare sonnets, the echoings and repetitions of sound are more immediately apparent than the latent metrical effects which I have tried to bring to light. [Here underlining, bold and italic bold type indicate each time a specific or related sound which is echoed: they do not mark metrical effects.]

> From <u>fai</u>rest creatures *we* desire in*crease*
> That <u>thereby</u> beauty's rose **might** <u>ne</u>ver **die**
> But as the <u>ri</u>per should **by** time de*cease*
> His <u>ten</u>der <u>heir</u> **might** <u>bear</u> his memory

Internal rhymes, '*we*...in*crease* / **might**...**die** / <u>ri</u>per...**by** time' '<u>ten</u>der <u>heir</u>...<u>bear</u>', convey pleasing patterns of eloquence which draw attention to relationships of meaning between the words – 'we' leads to 'increase'; 'riper' and 'time' seem to be (and are) connected; 'tender', 'heir' and 'bear' all seemingly fit together. There is a little logic of sound in each case, supporting the argument the lines present.

The opening of George Herbert's 'The Collar' is a maze and dazzle of rhymes and echoes and repetitions and related sounds, and tricks and plays upon orthography. Long lines become short ones by rhyming internally with the end rhyme-word and then, with a short line following, three lines read as two; alliteration comes and goes and the rhymes themselves are full-, near-, half-, eye- and assonantal rhymes. [My markings are once more for sound relationships only, not metre]

> I struck the **board** and *cried*. 'No **more**;
>> I will a**broad**!
> What? Shall I ever <u>sigh</u> and <u>pine</u>?
> <u>My lines</u> and <u>life</u> are free, free as the **road**
>> Loose as the *wind*, as large as **store**.
>>> Shall I be still in suit?
> Have I no harvest but a **thorn**
> To let me blood, and not re**store**
> What I have lost with cor**dial** fruit?
>>> **Sure** there was <u>wine</u>
>> Before <u>my sighs</u> did <u>dry</u> it: there was **corn**
>> Before <u>my</u> tears did drown it…

Within the masterful music of this, with consonants voicing their parts too, much of the echoing of vowels is just off-key, little slippages of off-rhyme like incidentals in music. The baroque intricacy and bravado of the art, however, serves the most serious and expressive of purposes.

'The Collar' sets out a dramatic challenge to God, the revolt of one who feels imprisoned in his clerical 'collar'. The power of the making, the proof of so much human skill over words shows the poet-speaker growing increasingly in charge at the same time as it allows a certain over-insistence to echo through his voicing of repeated sounds and patternings. His revolt, quite literally, sounds increasingly like self-justification as the initial anger gives way to a kind of display or performance. He holds the stage and must keep going; so long as he does not fluff his lines he might be all right; but the audience he addresses looks more and more like an audience of one, himself. When the poem does turn with its last four lines, it is the very way in which he hears his own voice which brings about the change. It is a poem about faith, submission to God, conscience but it is above all a poem about listening, about how words sound and what meanings sound makes. What the poet hears at the end, is another word within the insistent sounds he has toyed with – 'Child'. His own repetitions of the vowel sound in this word have prevented him from hearing the word itself: eventually, they have led to it being heard. This could be enough to end the argument and finish the poem but Herbert goes on. Brought back to an awareness that he is not alone, he takes up two more of the sounds which had formed his revolt and secures them again within a relationship to God. The harmony, within the cultural context the poem itself makes is, quite literally, an echo of the divine.

> Away! take heed;
> I will abroad.
> Call in thy death's head there; tie up thy fears.
> He that forbears
> To suit and serve his need
> Deserves his load.'
> But as I raved and grew more fierce and wild
> At every word,
> Methought I heard one calling, *Child!*
> And I replied, *My Lord.*

A poet of today would rarely aim to achieve the perfect resolution of such enclosing harmony. Fragmentation, discord, the provisional nature of artistic conclusion are all more likely to be revealed by the poem's close. The use of form, of the patterns and relationships which can be achieved by aural effects of metre and rhyme, rhythm and echoes of sound are no less crucial to the expressive purposes of the poem. The two last poems Keith Douglas sent to Betty Jesse before he set out for Normandy in 1944 show all the mastery he had acquired over rhyme. In the first of them, 'Mersa', the touch is so light, joining sounds with the slightest and least obvious of connections; making patterns of end-rhyme and internal rhyme which seem effortlessly made:

> This blue half circle of sea
> moving transparently
> on sand as pale as salt
> was Cleopatra's hotel:
>
> here is a guest house built
> and broken utterly since.
> An amorous modern prince
> lived in this scoured shell.
> ('Mersa')

The stanza form is quatrains; the rhyme-scheme shapes eight lines into a single octave: the verse, neat and fluent, is contained and extending, at once relaxed and concentrated. As Douglas had claimed in one of his first poems after action: 'Words are my instruments but not my servants /...There are those who capture them/ in hundreds, keep them prisoners.../ But I keep words only a breath of time / turning in the lightest of cages...' ['Words']. By the end of 'Mersa', the deadly observation at the poem's close will be made through a linking of consonant and a shift of vowel sound, no less deft than that in Herbert's 'The Collar':

> I see my feet like stones
> underwater, the logical little fish
> converge and nip the flesh
> imagining I am one of the dead.

We do not hear the final rhyme, because the sound which the word '*dead*' is echoing is a whole stanza away and it completed a sentence which, in the light of what is now being revealed, is long past : 'A dead tank alone / leans where the gossips *stood*. // I see my feet like stones...' Douglas has brought the formal pattern of his poem's rhyme scheme to completion, but the pattern of sounds which we actually attend to in this final stanza is the linking of 'logical' and 'little', 'fish' and flesh': the logic of sound enforcing a logic of nature which Darwin taught us and which offers no consolatory resolution, no means of escape from the reduced human significance the poem discovers through the action of the fish.

The other poem Douglas sent was, like this one, beautifully copied out in brightly coloured ink on vellum type paper, a present for Betty and another poem for her to give Tambi to publish. There is no suggestion that the text is incomplete, yet this poem ends without completing the pattern of rhyme sounds which it had subtly traced:

> The next month, then, is a window
> and with a crash I'll split the glass.
> Behind it stands one I must kiss,
> person of love or death
> a person or a wraith,
> I fear what I shall find.

It took me some time to realise that the final word in this last stanza of 'On a Return from Egypt' does actually rhyme, but not in sound: the form of the poem is completed with an eye-rhyme, a link between words which is orthographical and which we do not hear '*win*dow...*find*'. With a deftness of technique which is as compelling as the expressive function it performs, Douglas leaves us to look back to find, concealed within 'window' an honouring of the formal requirements of conventional rhyme, a hidden signature of his poetic mastery. We may then ponder the shift this eye-rhyme brings about, 'window...find': from the two syllabled feminine rhyme to the single syllable of a truncated feminine rhyme, or masculine rhyme; from a word with falling rhythm from stress to unstress, 'window' to the upbeat of a stress 'find' or to the suspense of an incomplete metrical foot: as if 'find' incorporates a tiny silence where its accompanying unstressed syllable should have been.

The dominant sound pattern of the close of the poem is left to the move as in 'Mersa', from consonant to echoing consonant, from 'fear' to 'find': the former word conditioning and transforming what should have been the revelation offered by the latter; this promises to be a finding which one would rather not accomplish. Divine intervention was not something Douglas anticipated when he sailed for Normandy and the liberation of mainland Europe. Unlike Herbert's, Douglas' patterning and harmonies have a distinctly secular and human origin. To the last though, he could use expressive form, could make the art of the poet convey meaning. The appearance of resolution, of completeness, of a final harmony, were things, at this stage, for which he would not allow his art to vouch.

4

The whole tendency through the primacy of discursive prose within our culture's texts over the past two centuries, has been towards a quest for unambiguous precision, a controlling and constraining of meaning. This has been particularly necessary through the rise of science and in order to counteract the development and expansion of the media with which to broadcast deceit. The poet's task has always been to combine precision, accuracy, unambiguity with a maximising of potential and unreliability – to disconcert the reader, to open up language, to make new things, to leave unsettled. The poet who wishes to control his text will therefore need the greatest care to ensure that it is properly punctuated: properly in the sense that it leaves open the meanings he wishes to leave open and cuts out the meanings he wishes to exclude. Such punctuation will include the indications of metre and sound patterning, line-ending and verse-form as well as the conventional signs for punctuating a text. One of the best compliments in the eyes of most poets is the response of their computer to their poems 'Too many errors to correct'. Poems thrive on flexibilities of syntax, multiple ambiguities, the redistribution and re-presentation of words, oddities and surprises. Much of the later stages of writing a poem is taken up by decisions as to where the poet wishes to have precision and where imprecision.

Within verse which is not rhymed and not strictly metrical, lineation can provide a kind of punctuation more flexible than the commas and question marks of current convention. Very simple examples, taken from a sequence I am currently writing, will demonstrate this at once. The following words cry out to be punctuated: 'must I take notice now you leap for me tell me how you stop'. To punctuate this conventionally would entail decisions among numerous possible readings: 'Must I take notice? Now you leap for me, tell me how you stop.' OR 'Must I take notice now you leap for me? Tell me how you stop.' OR 'Must I take notice now? You leap for me: tell me how you stop.'

Not using conventional punctuation but lineation it is possible too clarify the 'now' and potentially to keep all the other possibilities:

must I take notice
now you leap for me
tell me how you stop

Here is another simple example from the sequence, first, without lineation: 'not on your own perhaps your dear ones calling to the last and hearing all night long an answer it is there in the hand held out...' As my teachers who, rightly, could never follow my prose, would have asked: 'What exactly is in doubt here and who is calling and who is hearing whom? Are you perhaps not on your own, or are your dear ones perhaps calling to the

43

last?' My poem can answer as my prose could not – all these
and both and either and perhaps more:

> not on your own
> perhaps
> your dear ones
> calling to the last
> and hearing all night long
> an answer
> it is there
> in the hand held out
>   ('Heart work')

Ivor Gurney, we are told, could not punctuate. He uses full stops
where he need not. He lets a line run on to the next without
making clear what refers to what. He shifts prepositions in mid
sentence. As we read what he wrote, however, the punctuation
he uses or omits, along with his irregular or unresolved syntax,
opens up whole new possibilities within his words.

> Out of the heart's sickness the spirit wrote.
> For delight, or to escape hunger, or of war's worst anger.
> When the guns died to silence, and men would gather sense
> Somehow together, and find that this was life indeed.
>   ('War Books', *Selected Poems*, p.91)

Did the spirit write because of the heart's sickness or was that
sickness the matter of its writing? Or was it that the spirit could
write when away from the heart's sickness? The shifting possi-
bilities are slight but their irresolution brings the reader a sense
of tension, and more possible thoughts than resolution would
have brought. The second line's move from 'For' to 'to' to 'of'
and then another full stop, with no finite verb intervening, helps
alert us to other, unresolved, elements of the meanings: the
hunger sounds as if it is primarily that most literal hunger about
which Gurney often wrote in his letters from the trenches: but
the previous sentence had talked of 'spirit' and in the unsettled
verbal environment of these lines the word sounds like spiritual
hunger too. The meanings do not compete, the literal one remains
as firm as ever, but it is not secure.

Line-ending and punctuation mark have been made unreliable
as indicators of close or completeness: the reader reads these first
two lines with uncertainty, alternative possibilities, indecision.

Full stop and line ending, far from being markers of settled units of meaning are moments of pause, hesitation perhaps, gaps indicating that meaning is something which shifts as we go on, something accumulated, moved through and although momentarily so definite, something provisional. At the end of the third line the line-ending after the words 'gather sense' comes as an implicit comma but because there is no confirmation of this by the use of a comma, relationships can emerge which might have been muted. We can read: when the firing stops the men gather sense, they are somehow still together AND when the firing stops, the men somehow gather their senses together AND when the firing stops, the men somehow gather sense, a communal recovering of their nerves. It is the very unreliability of the punctuation in conventional terms which allows us to listen for other relationships, other meanings which could have been repressed by tighter controls. A whole cluster or bundle of meanings can be found, their very variety of nuance and emphasis portraying mixtures of feeling, mixtures of meaning.

The lines from Gurney which I have been discussing are in effect his answer to the questions which he had posed at the start of this poem, one of the many poems he composed in the asylum, 'War Books':

> What did they expect of our toil and extreme
> Hunger – the perfect drawing of a hearts dream?
> Did they look for a book of wrought art's perfection,
> Who promised no reading, nor praise nor publication?

The passion of these opening words takes us back to those matters discussed in the first of these lectures: the importance for the poet of support from editor, publisher, critic or literary friend. The place of 'wrought art's perfection', 'the perfect drawing of a heart's dream', the use of poetry itself, will be the subject of my final lecture.

III *No Less Than Bread*

'How easy it was to create poetry and write about poetry while it still existed'

(Tadeusz Różewicz)

1

Views of the nature and function of poetry change period to period, culture to culture. A turn of the century British view, given in brief quotations at the start of the anthology *Staying Alive* (2002), includes a persuasive definition by David Constantine: '[Poetry] is a widening of consciousness, an extension of humanity. We sense an ideal version when we read, and with it arm ourselves, to quarrel with reality' [p. 18]. This conception of poetry admirably expresses what many today turn to poetry for, and what for many, poetry does in their lives. Akhmatova's 1960 'Death of a Poet' [p. 81] offers an elegy no poet today would complain at: 'The unrepeatable voice won't speak again, /... And straightway it's grown quiet on the planet...'. She herself constructed a truly wonderful edifice out of her life and interaction with society as a poet. Her work and her life offer compellingly attractive evidence of what can be done with poems. From Akhmatova and, in particular, the epigraph she writes to her poem 'Requiem', the poet can still learn:

> In the fearful years of the Yezhov terror I spent seventeen months in prison queues in Leningrad. One day somebody "identified" me. Beside me, in the queue, there was a woman with blue lips. She had, of course, never heard of me; but she suddenly came out of that trance so common to us all and whispered in my ear (everybody spoke in whispers there): 'Can you describe this?' And I said: 'Yes, I can.' And then something like the shadow of a smile crossed what once had been her face. [p. 87]

To find words so as to bear witness, to tell what otherwise would be silenced, remains at the centre of the poet's task. In 1981, erecting the monument to the victims of Stalinism and

Russian occupation, the shipyard workers of Gdansk chose words from the poet Milosz for their inscription: 'You who harm the common man / crying out loud at his hurt / do not feel safe / the poet remembers / you may kill him / another will be born to bear witness...'. Today especially, we have to acknowledge that others too, remember and bear witness, that Milosz's term 'poet' may be extended to represent the spirit of poetry, the remembering and voicing of truths in resistance to political pressure in various forms: through prose, through performance, through the work of historians, film makers, journalists, archivists and the specifically focussed "whistle-blower". Poetry, in whatever sense, no longer has exclusive rights on bearing witness, if ever it had.

The specific art form poetry, represented by the poem, does have, however, special qualifications for taking part in this memorial and political task and performing it to effect. Through its use of rhythms and patterns the poem, whatever its prosody, possesses mnemonic, memorable quality. In aural cultures, poetry has generally been the form which preserves historical verbal memory, through chant and song and epic, and in the balances and patterned wording of proverb or riddle. Through this mnemonic quality poetry can be created and passed on without visible trace, without that evidence on which the censor and the secret policeman claim to depend. If the most obvious examples to us from the past century have been the secret role of poetry under the state terrorism of the Soviet Union and apartheid South Africa, poetry and its lyric accompaniment, song, have been worldwide a form of resistance and memory.

This memorial function is assisted by seemingly opposite poles of the poem's art: the poem's ability to make the most simple verbal patterns deeply meaningful, as in lyrics; and the poem's ability to use the most surprising or elaborate obliquity, as in fables, parables or extended metaphors and thus to say things which depend for their understanding on the reader's ability to translate them. The censor's difficulty with pinning down a poem's meaning is, in this way, the poet's and the reader's freedom.

It is not only for the purpose of inconveniencing censors that the poem makes it difficult to pin down its meaning: fluidities, indeterminacies, shifts of emphasis and a refusal to settle things are its natural environment. The poem draws attention to the words in which it is made: through the rhythmic markers of sound patterning and rhetorical structuring; through the visual markers of line-ending, stanza arrangement and the white spaces around it. It draws attention, also, through the simplicities or the novelties and strangeness of its use of words. It draws attention through its echoes and repetitions of whatever readers know from previous readings of poems or repeated readings of this one.

In Britain today, the term 'poetry' is still tossed between ignorant rejection of what it is supposed to stand for and reverent claims for what it is supposed to achieve. Among poets in public, there is something of a fashion first to belittle poetry, so as to gain the credibility of the street, and then to make pretentious claims about it, so as to attract the audience's admiration. The Hungarian poet Miklós Radnóti in his 'Second Eclogue' of 1941, cut through such pretensions: 'The poet writes, as dogs howl, or cats mew / Or small fish coyly spawn. What else am I to do?' [p. 32] Mickiewicz, Poland's 'national poet' brings us a further sense of perspective: 'It is more difficult to spend a day well than to write a book' [quoted by Różewicz (1982), p.11]. For the writer, of course, a day well spent may consist of writing a book; poetry for the writer of it is far too important to waste time getting engaged in cant about it. Osip Mandelstam, in a Soviet Union where everything was threatened by reductively materialist state policy and oppressive state terror, made the highest of claims for poetry, removing it at once from exclusivity and supposed competition to him: 'The people needed poetry no less than bread' [p. 13].

Coming from within the totalitarian regimes of the twentieth century such a claim, made by a poet who was to be murdered by the state specifically because of his poems, is worth our attention. Yet within a decade of Mandelstam's death, another view of poetry had grown which also traced its roots to the experience of totalitarianism:

> The dance of poetry came to an end during the Second World
> War in concentration camps created by totalitarian systems...
> [Różewicz, 1976 (1982, p. 13)]

It was no accident that [after the war] I chose to study history of art. I did it in order to...reconstruct man bit by bit...I was full of reverential wonder at works of art...but simultaneously I felt a growing contempt for all "aesthetic" values. I felt that something had come to an end for ever for me and for humanity.
[Różewicz, 1971 (1982, p. 11)]

How easy it was to create poetry and write about poetry while it still existed.
[Różewicz, 1959 (1976, p. 11)]

2

The views I have been quoting are central European and most are mid twentieth-century. In Britain we can hear a similar voice from a similar time and though we might not make the connection, he did:

I don't know if you have come across the word Bullshit – it is an army word and signifies humbug and unnecessary detail. It symbolises what I think must be got rid of – the mass of irrelevancies, of "attitudes", "approaches", propaganda, ivory towers, etc., that stands between us and our problems and what we have to do about them.

To write on the themes which have been concerning me lately in lyrical and abstract forms, would be immense bullshitting.
[*Poems*, p.134]

This is Keith Douglas, in Egypt in August 1943, one month after Tambimuttu's letter proposing a collection. He is writing to another editor, an acquaintance whose support and publication of his work had kept him going through 1942-43, J.C. Hall (whose support as editor/executor has continued to this day). Douglas is responding to a letter from Hall from London which expressed a preference for Douglas's earlier work over his recent poems from the North African battlefield. The first part of the letter has not survived, but in what we have, the opening words directly connect Douglas's new thinking to that of others: 'Incidentally you say I fail as a poet, when you mean I fail as a lyricist. Only someone who is out of touch, by which I mean first hand touch, with what has happened outside England – and from a cultural point of view I wish it had affected English life more – could make that criticism.' [p.134] Douglas returns to this context to connect his state of mind and poetic technique with a wider, continental European, view:

my object (and I don't give a damn about my duty as a poet) is to write true things, significant things in words each of which works for its place in the line. My rhythms, which you find enervated, are carefully chosen to be *read* as significant speech: I see no reason to be either musical or sonorous about things at present. When I do I shall be so again, and glad to. I suppose I reflect the cynicism and careful absence of expectation (it is not quite the same as apathy) with which I view the world. As many others to whom I have spoken, not only civilians and British soldiers, but Germans and Italians, are in the same state of mind, it is a true reflection. [pp.134-35]

Had Wilfred Owen drafted his famous 1918 Preface – 'Above all I am not concerned with Poetry' – in German or Polish, he would not, perhaps, have been sidelined for so long by academic literary history as an un-modern poet.

Douglas worked within a thoroughly British poetic tradition, taking much from the example of Rosenberg, Owen and his own Oxford tutor, Edmund Blunden. He brought to this tradition, from his conversations with Italian and German prisoners of war, from a reading of Rilke and Goethe (he collected himself a copy of Goethe's poems from a German gunpit), from an admiration for Aragon, from his time among refugees and exiles in cosmopolitan Palestine and Egypt, a continental European dimension.

Douglas's own terms: nothing sonorous or musical, no galleries of images, no irrelevancies of attitude, can be employed to trace the absences in Różewicz's anti-lyrics, which prove a test case for poetry's survival in the face of nihilism. Douglas writes of 'true things, significant things': Różewicz writes 'My objective was not poems, but facts.' [(1991) p.364] Douglas's 'cynicism' and 'careful absence of expectation' become in Różewicz, writing post-war, a loss not only of positive feelings but of meaning itself.

The Survivor

I am twenty-four
led to slaughter
I survived.

The following are empty synonyms:
man and beast
love and hate
friend and foe
darkness and light.

50

The way of killing men and beasts is the same
I've seen it:
truckfuls of chopped-up men
who will not be saved.

Ideas are mere words:
virtue and crime
truth and lies
beauty and ugliness
courage and cowardice.

Virtue and crime weigh the same
I've seen it:
in a man who was both
criminal and virtuous.

I seek a teacher and a master
may he restore my sight hearing and speech
may he again name objects and ideas
may he separate darkness from light.

I am twenty-four
led to slaughter
I survived.

[trs. Adam Czerniawski (1982) p.30]

The succession of plain statements rules out the increased
expectations which the reader has brought to poetry from the
Romantics on – expectations of beauty, of transcendence, of
imaginative reach and complexity of meaning. The meanings
here are complex, but in the manner of an untieable knot rather
than that of a code or treasure map. Even the irony which ought
to lie behind the poem and enable the reader to take its negatives
as a challenge is denied leverage by the flatness of tone; these
are facts, I have survived. The cultural terms of ethics, religion
and myth, the discriminations implied within language have
lost their established meanings, their connections to a world of
human thought broken. There are allusions, in the sixth stanza,
to religion, to Jesus' curing of blindness, to Adam's naming of
creatures and to the creation story of Genesis. They trace an
undoing of supposed progress, to before these things, before
even God's intervention.

Physically, however, this looks like a poem. It has stanzas,
line-endings, balance of word and phrase, timed repetitions and

a structure which takes the first stanza and repeats it as the last. These visual and rhetorical declarations that this is a poem, define the nature of the significance which the work's statements have here. Had they been simply spoken to us by someone they would arouse a pained desire somehow to help that person; were they in a journal, we would read them with gratitude for their honesty and hope the writer found some way out. Written out as prose – well, written out as prose, with no word changed and no further context, the surviving features in them would lead us to read them as a prose poem. Here, as a poem, the statements reach us in a condition of suspense. They are not exactly provisional, certainly here they are not qualified, but they are exposed for our attention as if in invisible quotes. These invisible quotes leave us ponder what they contain; to measure the absolutes of the statements of the poem beside what else we know; to start our questions.

3

Miklós Radnóti was well established as a writer through the 1930s in Hungary; a poet who admired Lorca and took particular political interest in the Spanish Civil War. In the early years of the Second World War, as a Jew in Hungary he suffered racial oppression in addition to the threats of war's violence. His response as poet was to write poems based on the Classical model provided by Virgil, eclogues: as civilised, formal and remote an environment as poetry could find. As well as following his Roman predecessor in the use of prosody, he followed the topics of his debates and concerns, meditating on the ways of the world and its powers, using dialogue form. The settings and speakers of Radnóti's eclogues, however, were self-evidently up to date.

My earlier quotation about the creaturely naturalness of writing poetry, was dated by Radnóti 27 April 1941. The poet's interlocutor in that eclogue is a bomber pilot, a pilot who was intoxicated with battle in the air and boastful of his power, telling the poet: 'And tomorrow, this craven Europe shall know / Fear in their air-raid shelters, as they tremble hidden away.../ But enough of that, let's leave it. Have you written since yesterday?' [p.32]. Vanity has led the airman to make his enquiry.

The poet's response – he writes 'as dogs howl, or cats mew' etc – is therefore not just an insistence on the naturalness of writing for the poet, but an insistence on the poet's viewpoint; a refusal to be inveigled into the killer's way of seeing and speaking.

Radnóti elaborates on the poet's terms: 'I write about everything – write even for you, up there, / So that flying you may know of my life and how I fare / ...When the city squares bulge, all of them terror-stricken, / Breathing stops, and even the sky seems to sicken, / ...And the planes keep coming on...'. The poet's imagination instructs the pilot in the consequences of the pilot's actions. He then repeats his own words about poetry, but with dismissive impatience: 'Poet's write, / Cats mew, dogs howl, small fish...and so on; but you who fight, / What do you know? Nothing. You listen, but all you hear / Is the plane.'

By the end of the eclogue the pilot's wish for the poet's approbation has shifted power from himself to the poet, he confesses to his own fears and pleads with the poet: 'But you know and will write about it! It won't be a secret that I, / Who now just destroy, homeless between the earth and the sky, / Lived as a man lives. Alas, who'd understand or believe it? / Will you write of me?' [p.33]. The poet does not refuse the request. With a dark humour characteristic of his work, Radnóti has already written the pilot's poem within the preceding eclogue, though it is not the poem the pilot would have wanted. The words the poet actually chooses for his response to the request for a poem, make no compromise and define the terms on which the writing of poetry depends: 'If I live, if there's anyone left to read it.'

Radnóti retained the power to write with such sharpness of mind even when his situation worsened. After two periods of forced labour, in mid 1944 he was imprisoned in a slave labour camp in northern Serbia, near Bor. He continued to write eclogues. The pastoral setting – a remote place, a rural retreat removed from civilised life, according to custom – is 'Lager Heideman'. The 'Seventh Eclogue', dated July 1944 by Radnóti, describes this place of barbed wire, shaven-headed men in rags, their inhuman exhaustion and their last vestiges of life: their homesickness, sleeping or waking dreams of before and elsewhere. Again, such 'thoughts of elsewhere' accord with the conventions of 'eclogue', and they are given creative respect. This eclogue, however, is not specifically in dialogue form: instead it is cast as an imaginary letter sustaining a conversation; the interlocutor, this time, is the poet's wife as he carries her in his mind. Once again, in the course of the poem the question of poetry's survival and its place in all of this arises. This time it is the poet himself who asks it:

> Is there a land still, tell me, where this verse form has meaning?
>
> Without putting in the accents, just groping line after line,
> I write this poem here, in the dark, just as I live,
> Half-blind, like a caterpillar inching my way across paper;
> Torches, books – the *Lager* guards took everything;
> And no post comes – just fog that settles upon the barracks.
> [p.47]

The poem's continuation, with its orderly thoughts and artistic shaping sustained through to the end provide an unspoken response. The close of the poem plays on an old motif of the love poet – the poet dying from separation from his love. He addresses his wife: 'I can no longer die without you, nor can I live'.

From August to October, the Russian armies advancing, Radnóti and the other camp inmates were sent on a forced march, on which any prisoner showing signs of being unable to continue was shot. On Radnóti's body, when it was eventually disinterred from a roadside, there was the notebook which contained his latest eclogues, and a small group of similarly pastoral poems, written on the march. In this group Radnóti again adapted a form, a non-literary one this time, but a modern descendant of the pastoral, the postcard. In these 'Postcards' he sends vivid pictures giving news of where he is. The postcards, like the pictures of earlier artist's depictions of the ravages of war, show the brutality and apocalyptic fire and smoke of his surroundings: 'Blood-red, the spittle drools from the oxen's mouths; / The men, stooping to urinate, pass blood' [p.58]. 'No more than six or seven miles away / Haystacks and houses flare; / There, on the meadows' verges, crouch the swains, / Pipe-smoking, dumb with fear.' [p.57]

The setting has remained pastoral, though war has transformed the components of the scene; war travesties of the literary form's rural world. These six or seven miles from the battle, however, a place of terrified anticipation for the peasants, for the poet is still distance enough to perceive how the world of peace appears: there is a lake, some sheep, a girl tending them. Radnóti's imagination takes hold of this and for one moment sets beside war's powers of metamorphosis, those of the poet: 'Here still, where the tiny shepherdess steps in, / Ripples on the lake spread; / A flock of ruffled sheep bend over it / And drink the clouds they tread.' [p.57]

In this 'Postcard' the creative mind's ability to refuse to be silenced by the nihilism of war's evidence is, for the poem's duration, proved. Another poem from Radnóti's notebook, 'Forced March', returns to a different manifestation of the mind's creative capacity, the fevered homesickness and daydreams of the men in his 'Seventh Eclogue' from Lager Heideman. 'Forced March', dated 15 September 1944, makes clear immediately what is at stake: 'A fool he is who, collapsed, rises and walks again...', and for ten lines, each poised and formally written, with a classical 'caesura', break in its middle, he elaborates on why this is so:

> Yet he, as if wings uplifted him,   sets out on his way,
> And in vain the ditch calls him   back, who dare not stay.
> And if asked why not, he might answer   – without leaving his path –
> That his wife was awaiting him,   and a saner, more beautiful death.
> Poor fool! He's out of his mind...
> [p. 56]

This knowledge is powerless, however, to stop his longing: 'O if only I could believe that everything of worth / Were not just in my heart – that I still had a home on earth; / If only I had...'. The yearning leads his mind to conjure what could, if only he still had a home on earth, be true:

> ...As before,   jam made fresh from the plum
> Would cool on the old verandah,   in peace the bee would hum,
> An end-of-summer stillness   would bask in the drowsy garden,
> Naked among the leaves   would sway the fruit trees' burden,
> And she would be waiting, blonde   against the russet hedgerow,
> As the slow morning painted   slow shadow over shadow...

Radnóti had written of an orchard garden and fruit and the season, in a poem of 1936, 'A Mountain Garden'. There, 'Summer has fallen asleep...a late flower stands / Naked and half-alive';

he heard 'the sound / Of a withered apricot-bough crack over-head / To sink its own weight slowly to the ground.' 'Late too, a golden bee / Is flying a death-circle around my head'. At that time and in that poem, awareness of oncoming war had given the season's move towards autumn a specific, dark foreboding. As the garden's fruit was proffered 'to the heavy season of the dead' he had asked: '…as for you, young man, what mode of death awaits you? / Will a shot hum like a beetle towards your heart, / Or a loud bomb rend the earth…your young flesh torn apart?' [p.17]

'Forced March' repeats the materials and the shape of these thoughts but it moves in an opposite direction. Instead of the stability and presence of the garden, the garden is a distant memory transformed into an idyll through the intensity of his desperation. Instead of fears of loss and imaginings of possible death, there is the fact that he is about to be killed. Instead of breaking off the fancy conjured by the autumn garden with the realisation of death, his daydream in 'Forced March' must be elaborated on, extended as far as possible so that it can grow into an overwhelming reality in his mind. Thus alerted, his mind can find potential again in the outer world, a different version of reality from that which war proposes: 'As the slow morning painted slow shadow over shadow / Could it perhaps still be? The moon tonight's so round! / Don't leave me friend, shout at me: I'll get up off the ground!' The power of the imagination, literally, can save life.

<h1 align="center">4</h1>

Before David Jones finally asserts the authority of the 'geste' and 'the man who was on the field…and who wrote the book' he takes us through a most elaborate journey. From the title page which carries its own epigraph from Welsh epic we move through a series of marked entrances: a dedicatory inscription to soldiers of both sides, a further epigraph with a page to itself, from Mandeville – 'Evil betide me if I do not open the door…'; then a further title page, for 'PART I', with its own title, 'The many men so beautiful', itself a quotation, and yet another epigraph, translated from the epic in Welsh, *Y Gododdin*. In effect we have opened a sequence of doors, moving in stages from our starting point, back into legend and history, across cultures and languages and at each point perceiving words which are exposed as title or quotation or signs on an inscription, placed there for the occasion, ceremonial or even liturgical in their effect.

Beside such mysteries, there is the friendly helpfulness of first, a 'Note of Introduction' by T.S. Eliot commending the book to us, then a most straightforward Author's Preface: all of this supported by fascinating and informative notes at the back of the book, giving sources and further details. Our progress is like the move towards an inner sanctum, at the same time as we have the backwards and sideways moves through the notes to other texts and opinions. When we actually arrive at the opening words of the text itself – or has it already started with the epigraphs – we meet a very unholy place: a parade ground, with its barrack-room humour and a hero who lacks the proper equipment: "O1 Ball', 'Ball of No 1' [p.1]. Jones, like Blunden before him, bemoaned the legal impossibility of reproducing in print the actual obscenity and blasphemy of the soldier's natural speech in the trenches. His jokes and wit, his play on the speech of different classes and individuals and regions of Britain, direct us to recognise the existence of a different language which he cannot use: 'Pick 'em up, pick 'em up – I'll stalk within yer chamber' – brilliantly Jones plays on Wyatt's erotic poem 'They Flee From Me' to make an equivalent for the parade sergeant's obscene wit. Without the censors we would lose such delights, but Jones's ever present play on registers and modes of speech would then, presumably, have had an even wider range. As it is there is little doubt as to the way of life of the people and the nature of events his words are shadowing:

> Wastebottom married a wife on his Draft-leave but the whinnying splinter razored diagonal and mess-tin fragments drove inward and toxined underwear.
> He maintained correct alignment with the others, face down, and you never would have guessed. [...]

> Talacryn doesn't take it like Wastebottom, he leaps up & says he's dead, a-slither down the pale face – his limbs a-girandole at the bottom of the nullah,
> but the mechanism slackens, unfed
> and he is quite still
> which leaves five paces between you and the next live one to the left.
>   [pp. 157-58]

In this remarkable counterpoint, concord and discord of modes of speech and written expression portray for us over the span of *In Parenthesis* as near to an unforgettable image of the details of the trench soldier's existence as our forgetful minds can manage. Jones' ear for nuance of diction and speech builds from word to word and phrase to phrase a plenitude, a richness of creativity which does have a Shakespearean breadth to it: the sound or feel of a mess tin against you; the timing of anxiety shifting to fear then terror; the telling, innocently made gesture as the sergeant licks his indelible pencil, or the colonel parts his moustache with the tip of his. Jones, in the opening words of his Preface, writes with truth about his purpose – 'This writing has to do with some things I saw, felt, & was part of.' [p.ix]; the precision of these modest claims ensures our assent. Such is the power of his work and its effect, when we reach the end of it we may well have forgotten other, equally exact definitions of the nature and compass of his writing given in his introductory remarks.

The course of Jones's narrative continues the progressive, inward movement his epigraphs and title pages achieved from the first. We move, with his soldiers, from parade ground, through embarkation, to first weeks in France, time in the trenches, time under fire; and then, in the final part, Part 7, step by step we move in slow motion, as the soldier's fears move him, through the hours of waiting to the moment of 'going over the top' and then on, into the midst of battle. The narrative ends with the wounding of the hero, 'O1 Ball' and his removal from the battlefield. The polyphony of voices which have brought us through this action, reach their climax and fade to a final elegy:

But why dont the bastards come –
Bearers! stret-cher bear-errs!
or do they divide the spoils at the Aid-Post.
    But how many men do you suppose could bear away a third of us:
drag just a little further – he may yet counter-attack,

Lie still under the oak
next to the Jerry
and Sergeant Jerry Coke.
    The feet of the reserves going up tread level with your forehead; and no word for you; they whisper one with another;

pass on, inward;
these latest succours:
green Kimmerii to bear up the war.

Oeth and Annoeth's hosts they were
who in that night grew
younger men
younger striplings.

[p.187]

The new men are 'green Kimmerii', Welsh troops, named thus
to evoke their ancient warrior heritage. They are also the latest
suckers, 'green' in military terms. In the legend of 'Oeth and
Annoeth's hosts', a ghostly army added to your numbers: here
they are the new, conscript army, not yet full grown, even more
shockingly unsuited for death than the veterans they replace.
Jones's artistic integrity, has ensured through these references
that we are aware his narrative is not the end of the story; that
after all the losses he has depicted, this new army will face the
remorselessness of war. Jones then concludes with the words
on which these lectures opened: 'The geste says this and the
man who was on the field…and who wrote the book…the man
who does not know this has not understood anything.[48]'

If we follow up the reference in note '48' we will learn much
about Jones's methods of adaptation and appropriation of sources
but little to help us conclude what it is the geste says. Extracted
from René Hague's free translation the words, when fitted back
as far as is possible into their original occurrence in Ronsard's
Chanson de Roland, are spoken by the poet narrator to reassure
the audience about the accuracy of huge claims he has just made,
to convince the listener that there actually were four hundred
men, 'mostly wounded and headless', around the slain Bishop
Turpin; a fact which proved just how many men this great
warrior brought down on his way to his own death. The words
in Ronsard are used in passing; Jones's imagination has seized
on their ability to hold a powerful concluding resonance. Placed
at the end of his narrative they are made a reminder to the
reader that he must attend to the report of the witness with
the greatest care, grant his words hearing and belief so that he
may learn something he could not otherwise have known. That
mysterious 'this' then, can be taken to mean 'what my book

has said', 'what the text says' – attend to that or you will not have understood anything. Such words would make a fine close to every piece of writing: attend to the text, go back to it and listen with the utmost care, otherwise it will not lead you to anything. But this is not all that the final lines have said. They have returned the story to the insider knowledge of 'the man who was on the field' and to the privacy of authorial experience. They present a resonant claim to attention, a movement away from the reader, and a conundrum.

Jones took from the *Chanson de Roland* and from *Y Gododdin* precedents for his epic lament for dead comrades. His Inscription dedicates his book to these comrades, including those on the other side: 'THE ENEMY FRONT-FIGHTERS WHO SHARED OUR PAINS AGAINST WHOM WE FOUND OURSELVES BY MISADVENTURE'. The generosity of such words is a measure of the pacific and humane memorial his poem sets up. These very pacific purposes, however, involve exclusions. Minded of the men lost in Ronsard and *Y Gododdin*, we realise that participation in battle there is honoured not only for its comradeship and endurance but more frequently for the soldier's ferocity in battle. Jones, like so many war memorials put up all over Europe around the time of his writing, honours his soldiers for losing their lives, with no mention of killing others.

Keith Douglas observed to someone who asked him to cut from his narrative (*Alamein to Zem Zem*) references he made to the soldiers' delight in 'loot' taken from the battlefield: 'I'm not sure the instinct for selectivity isn't based on sentimentality, anyhow.' [*Letters*, pp. 342-43] Jones' selectivity could be called, in a profound sense, sentimentality. His love towards the dead led him to protect them by omitting evidence which might damage their reputation as honourable victims. In fact, Jones, by design, omitted very much more than this particular evidence, as he makes clear in his preface: 'The period covered begins early in December 1915 and ends in July 1916. The first date corresponds to my going to France. The latter roughly marks a change in the character of our lives in the Infantry on the West Front. From then onward things hardened into a more relentless, mechanical affair, took on a more sinister aspect.' [p.ix] Jones has stopped as the Somme battle starts, the battle which, for the British, is the defining point in the communal memory of that war. His text is partial, highly selective, more extremely and openly so than many texts, as is indicated by his title: this narrative is no more than a parenthesis, something between what went before and what followed.

For the reader, every poem is a parenthesis – or, within my chosen image, in quotation marks. The reader must first attend to every word and pattern within it, try, as far as he can, to listen as accurately and fully as possible to what it says, following all the selections it has made and indicated visibly and invisibly. Then the reader must look to either side of what the poet has selected in making the text. For the writer, at the poem's end there is, however temporarily, a full stop. For the reader, whatever his eyes see or the editor indicates, there is always a question mark.

A NOTE ON SOURCES

I *Opening the Door*

Keith Douglas: *The Letters* (Carcanet, 2000), *A Prose Miscellany* (Carcanet, 1985), *Complete Poems* (OUP, 1978).
Wilfred Owen: *The Collected Letters* (1967), *The Complete Poems and Fragments* (1983).
Isaac Rosenberg: *The Collected Works* (1937).
Elaine Feinstein: *Anna of All the Russias: The Life of Anna Akhmatova* (2005); also Anna Akhmatova: *Selected Poems* (Bloodaxe Books, 1989), trans. Richard McKane.

II *The Unheard Prompter*

The Oxford Shakespeare, Cornell Wordsworth and Oxford Herbert.
Brennan O'Donnell: *The Passion of Wordsworth's Metrical Art* (Ohio, 1995).
Ivor Gurney: *Selected Poems*, ed. George Walter (1996); see also Ivor Gurney: *Best Poems and The Book of Five Makings* (1995).
Douglas as above.
Desmond Graham: *Heart work* (Flambard Press, 2007)

III *No Less Than Bread*

Osip Mandelstam: *Selected Poems* (Penguin Books, 1977), trans. Clarence Brown and W.S. Merwin.
Anna Akhmatova: *Selected Poems* (1988), trans. D.M.Thomas.
Tadeusz Rózewicz: *Selected Poems* (Penguin Books, 1976) and *Conversations with the Prince and other poems* (Anvil Press, 1982), both trans. Adam Czerniawski; also Tadeusz Rózewicz's prose in *The Poetry of Survival*, ed. Daniel Weissbort (1991).
Miklós Radnóti: *Forced March: Selected Poems*, trans. Clive Wilmer and George Gömöri (Carcanet, 1979).
David Jones: *In Parenthesis* (Faber and Faber, 1937).

Desmond Graham was born in 1940 in Cobham, Surrey. He studied English at Leeds, at the time when Geoffrey Hill lectured there, Jon Silkin was poet in residence and Tony Harrison, a graduate student. Harrison passed on the editorship of *Poetry and Audience* to him and there, he published for the first time, work by the undergraduate Ken Smith. After lecturing in Germany and Africa, he returned to Leeds in 1966 to complete a PhD on Keith Douglas. He was visiting lecturer at Munich University (1968-70), Mannheim University (1970-71) and in 1971 moved to a Lectureship in English at Newcastle University. He is Emeritus Professor of Poetry there, and lives in Newcastle and southern Germany.

The lectures he gave in Africa were published as *Introduction to Poetry* (OUP, 1969). His work on Keith Douglas as biographer and editor appeared over the next ten years: *Keith Douglas 1920-1944: A Biography* (OUP, 1974); *Keith Douglas: The Complete Poems* (OUP, 1978; Faber, 2000); *Alamein to Zem Zem* (OUP, 1979); and, later, in *Keith Douglas: A Prose Miscellany* (Carcanet, 1985) and *The Letters* (Carcanet, 2000). His critical work on First World War poets was published as *The Truth of War: Owen, Blunden and Rosenberg* (Carcanet, 1984) and an extensive essay on Ivor Gurney in *The Ivor Gurney Society Journal 2001*.

From 1980 he returned to his own poetry. He was in *Ten North-East Poets* (Bloodaxe Books, 1980), regularly reviewed poetry for *Stand* and won prizes in the National, Arvon and Cardiff competitions. In 1989 the winning of the Seren International Poetry Competition led to inclusion in the four-man selection, *Seren Poets 2* (1990). Villa Vic Press published (in conjunction with concert performances in Germany and England) *A Set of Signs for Chopin's Twenty Four Preludes* (1990); and *A Rumtopf for Summer* (1990). In 1993 Seren published his first full collection, *The Lie of Horizons*. This was followed by *The Marching Bands* (Seren, 1996), *Not Falling* (Seren, 1999), *After Shakespeare* (Flambard, 2001) and *Milena Poems* (Flambard, 2003).

His long connections with Germany and, since 1984, with Poland, led to *Poetry of the Second World War: An International Anthology* (Chatto, 1995; Pimlico, 1998), and his co-translation of the Polish poet Anna Kamienska, *Two Darknesses: Selected Poems* (Flambard, 1994); currently he is co-translating Julia

Hartwig. His *After Shakespeare* was translated into Polish as *Cien Makbeta* [Macbeth's Shadow] (Gdansk, 2001) and a collected translation of his poems about Poland is in progress. His book-length sequence of poems *Heart work* is published by Flambard in May 2007.